kansas:
our pioneer heritage

by
Dr. Robert N. Manley

Lincoln, Nebraska

Library of Congress Catalog Card No. 81—82-81541
ISBN: 0-939644-03-7

For Sarah, Stephanie and Bobby, and all the children of Kansas.

Cover Design by Steve Baxter
Illustrations by Al Heilig and Russ Wall
First edition—First printing
Printed in United States of America

kansas:
our pioneer heritage

Table of Contents

Dr. Robert Manley

Hello, boys and girls. I want to talk with you for just a minute about this book I've written for you.

First of all, this is a book about Kansas. As you read my book I know you will discover that Kansas has an exciting past. You will also find out that the history of Kansas is the story of people—people who were just like you and me.

And you will discover that there is history in every part of Kansas. In every town and city, on every farm and ranch in Kansas, there is history just waiting to be found!

Don't be surprised if some of the best stories you find are about people in your own family. Your family is a very important part of history.

There are two things you need to remember. First, remember that history is the story of people, all kinds of people. Second, remember that history is around you no matter where you live in Kansas.

I hope you will enjoy reading my book. I know you will have fun as you learn about Kansas, the State where you live.

The title of this book is

KANSAS:
OUR PIONEER HERITAGE

Now I want to ask you a question: what is a pioneer?

Not long ago I asked a class of Kansas students that question. Timmy was the first to raise his hand.

"Dr. Manley, pioneers were men and women who came to Kansas years ago. They were the first settlers in Kansas."

Kim thought for a moment and then she said, "The explorers and fur traders were pioneers, weren't they?"

"What about the soldiers who lived in the Army posts along the Santa Fe Trail?" asked Becky. "They were pioneers, too."

Joy raised her hand. "The farmers who plowed the sod and planted the first crops were important Kansas pioneers. I'm sure of that!"

I could tell that Angie had some other pioneers in mind. I asked her to tell us whom she was thinking about.

"Well," she said slowly, "I think the men and women who built towns in Kansas were pioneers."

Then Bill called out from the back of the room. He was so excited he didn't even raise his hand before he spoke.

"I know one group of pioneers we shouldn't forget! How about the cowboys who drove the Texas longhorns up the trail to Abilene and Dodge City? They were real Kansas pioneers," declared Bill.

The students had some good answers for my question, didn't they? They told me about some interesting Kansas pioneers.

Can you think of some pioneers the students didn't tell me about? What other Kansas pioneers can you think of?

Now I want to ask **you** a question.

Why were the pioneers of Kansas important?

Here is the answer. Pioneers were important because they prepared the way for those of you who live in Kansas today.

Here is how the dictionary defines the word "pioneer": **A pioneer is a person who prepares the way for others.**

Pioneers drove their covered wagons along the Kansas trails. Today modern highways follow the old pioneer trails.

Pioneers built the towns and cities where many Kansans live today.

They plowed the sod and made farms. Many Kansas families live on farms that were made by their pioneer ancestors.

Then there were the pioneer cattlemen who had ranches in Kansas. Fat cattle still graze on the rich Kansas grasslands.

THESE ARE SOME OF THE WAYS THE PIONEERS PREPARED THE WAY FOR YOU!

A Kansas Pioneer, Amelia Earhart
Amelia Earhart was born in Atchison, Kansas. She was one of the first women aviators in America; and she was the first woman to fly across the Atlantic Ocean.

Now that you understand the word **pioneer** we can get started. This book is going to tell you about some very special pioneers. You are going to learn about the pioneers who built Kansas. And remember: These Kansas pioneers prepared the way for you.

UNIT ONE:

ON YOUR MARK

In this unit you will meet a Kansas pioneer with an unusual name.

You will also learn about Kansas, the land of the pioneers.

Chapter One:
The Story of Johnny Jayhawk

The huge steamboat slowly chugged up the muddy Missouri River.

Billows of black smoke belched from the smokestacks of the steamboat. Every few minutes the steam whistle let off a blast that echoed up and down the wide river.

Three children, two girls and a boy, stood at the railing of the boat. They were watching the dark, brown water as it bubbled along the side of the boat.

The two girls didn't look very happy.

"Why, oh, why, did Mother and Father decide to leave St. Louis?" Sarah said loudly. "Look out there." She pointed to the banks of the river. "There's nothing out here but trees and prairies and a few dumb looking little towns."

Her sister Stephanie nodded. "I just can't imagine we'll have any fun in the place where we are going to live. By the way, Sarah, where **are** we going?"

Sarah put her arm around her sister and replied, "We're going to a place called Kansas." And both the girls began to cry softly.

But Bobby, their brother, didn't cry. No, he was busy watching the shore. And all the time Bobby was thinking, "I'll bet Kansas isn't so bad. It will be fun to live in a new country where there are Indians and soldiers and cowboys and all sorts of pioneers. I'm glad we're going to Kansas!"

It was June, 1861, and this family was on their way to the new state of Kansas.

Many other people were going to Kansas at this time. Some were going in hopes of making lots of money. Others were just curious about the country. They wanted to know what Kansas was like. Some wanted land to farm. Many of the people wanted to help build new towns.

There were also those who came to Kansas to help keep it a **free state** — that is, a state where it would be against the law to own slaves.

Sarah, Stephanie and Bobby knew that there was a terrible war going on. Back in St. Louis there were blue-coated soldiers all over the place.

They remembered the night Father told Mother that they might move to Kansas. And they remembered that Mother cried out, "I will not take the children to "bleeding Kansas"!

Father said, "Yes, it is true that there has been terrible, bloody fighting in Kansas. But Kansas is now a free state, and there are great opportunities in that new country."

So, the family packed their belongings, boarded the steamboat and left St. Louis. Their next stop was Atchison, Kansas.

For ten days the steamboat struggled up the Missouri River. Then, early in the morning, Father called to Mother and the children to join him on deck.

"Look up ahead, children," Father called out. "There is Atchison, our future home!"

The boat's whistle let out a long, loud shriek! The engines slowed down, and the big boat slowly moved toward the shore.

Hundreds of people lined the river. They waved and called out to friends on the boat.

Behind the crowd lay Atchison. There were two or three dirt streets and a few wooden buildings. Atchison in 1861 wasn't much of a city.

The steamboat gave a big bump as it ran aground. Ropes were thrown from the boat to men on the land who tied the boat up to strong posts. Then wooden planks were laid between the boat and the land. The people began to walk ashore.

"Here we are in our new home," declared Mother. "This is Kansas, the land of the jayhawks!"

"Jayhawks?" cried the three children all at the same time. "What are jayhawks?"

Father laughed. "If you'll stand still for just a moment I'll tell you."

"Children, a few years ago there was a great deal of bloody fighting in Kansas. Men who wanted to have slaves in Kansas fought against men who wanted Kansas to be a free state.

"It's said that an Irishman lived in southeastern Kansas where the fighting went on all the time. One day, this Irishman, who was a free-state man, was seen walking briskly down the road. A neighbor called out to him and asked, 'Pat, where have ye been' "

"As a matter of fact, Pat was just returning from a raid upon some pro-slavery settlers from Missouri. 'Well,' Pat called out cheerfully, 'I've been jayhawking! You see, back in Ireland we have a bird we call the jayhawk. It catches little birds and then plays with them just as a cat plays with a mouse it has caught. I've been doing the same thing myself. I've been **playing** with the boys from Missouri!'

"So from that time on," Father concluded, "Kansas has been known as the land of the jayhawks!"

Now I would like you to meet an imaginary friend of mine. His name is Johnny Jayhawk, and Johnny has something to say to you.

"Hi, boys and girls. My name is Johnny Jayhawk. I came to Kansas back in pioneer days when life was not always easy."

"I want to help you learn about Kansas, so you can be proud of our State, just as I am. Follow me and I'll tell you about the pioneers of Kansas who prepared the way for you!"

Chapter Two
Kansas-Land of the Pioneers

Kansas is the name of the State where you live.

Do you know what the word "Kansas" means?

Kansas is named for the Kansa Indians. The name "Kansa" means "south wind people."

A Kansa Indian. The State of Kansas is named for the Kansa tribe.

Kansas is one State in our country, the United States of America. Can you find Kansas on this map of our country?

There are many historical markers in Kansas. These markers tell us interesting and important stories about the people and the places of Kansas.

I am standing by a very interesting historical marker.

It is located in Smith County not far from the town of Lebanon.

Do you know why this marker is important?

The marker stands in the exact geographical center of the United States.

Let's find out some other things about Kansas.

How large is Kansas? The map below will show you.

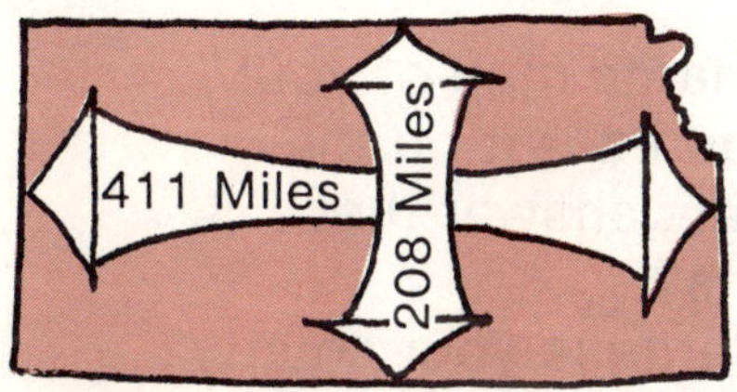

Now let's compare the size of Kansas with some other States.

Which State is larger, Texas or Kansas?

Which is larger, Kansas or Rhode Island?

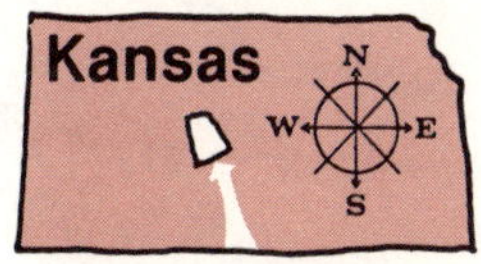

Which is larger, California or Kansas?

The map below shows the counties of Kansas.

How many counties are there in Kansas?

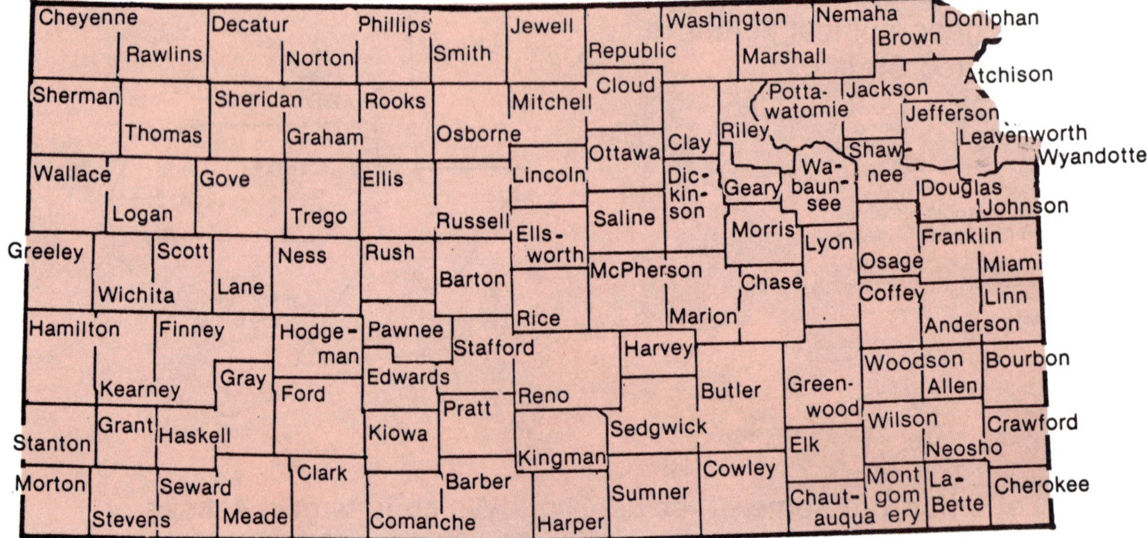

What is the name of the county where you live?

Get a large map of your county and put it on the wall. Then, answer these questions?

1. How large is your county?
2. What is the county seat of your county?
3. How did your county get its name?

HERITAGE SPECIAL HERITAGE SPECIAL HERITAGE SPECIAL HERITAGE SPECIAL

Highways Of History

Some modern Kansas highways follow old and important pioneer trails. Look at the map below and find the pioneer trails and the modern Kansas highways.

* The Santa Fe trail. Today U.S. highway 56 follows much of the route of that important pioneer trail.

* Cannonball Stage Coach Road. This road was named for Cannonball Green, who drove the stage over this route. Today U.S. 54 follows that well-known road.

* The Chisholm trail brought thousands of Texas longhorns to Abilene. You can follow that famous cattle trail by driving on U.S. 81 and Kansas highway 15.

* You have heard of the Pony Express. In northeastern Kansas U.S. highway 36 runs very close to the route over which these famous riders galloped their ponies.

* In the 1850's soldiers marched between Fort Leavenworth and Fort Scott over what was known as a military road. Actually the "road" was little more than a trail. Today U.S. 69 follows that old military road.

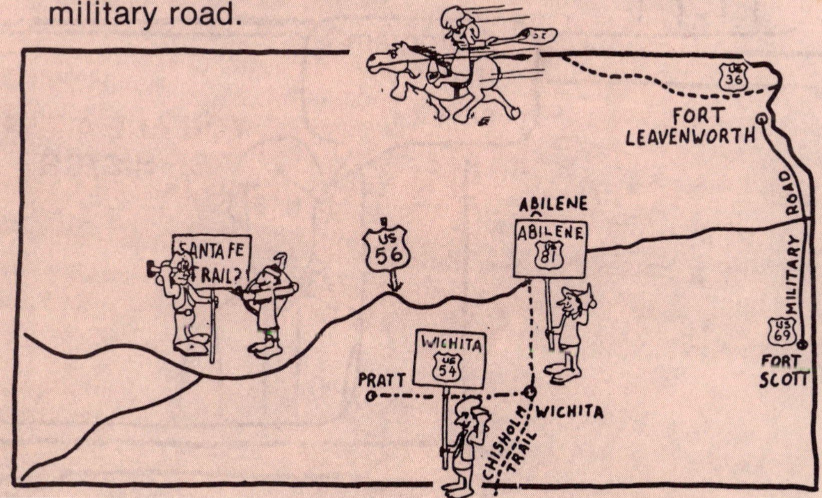

HERITAGE SPECIAL HERITAGE SPECIAL HERITAGE SPECIAL HERITAGE SPECIAL

UNIT TWO: OUR EXCITING PAST

Chapter Three:
History and Heritage

Please think about the word "history" for a minute. What does the word "history" mean to you?

Listen as some students tell us what the word "history" means to them.

"History is the story of the past. It is the story of pioneers who lived in log cabins and traveled in covered wagons."

"I know what history is! History is the story of famous people, such as George and Martha Washington. They were very famous people in American history. He was the first President of the United States."

"I'll tell you what history is! History tells us about important things that happened in the past. Such as the first time men flew in an airplane. That is history!"

Those are very good answers to the question, "What is history?" History does tell us about the past. History also tells us about famous people and important events that happened in the past.

But history is something else. Listen to our friend, Johnny Jayhawk:

"HISTORY IS THE STORY OF PEOPLE"

Now listen carefully.

The first thing you should know about history is that it is the story of people, all kinds of people.

This means that history includes the story of you and your family.

You must not think that history is the story of **other** people. Don't be like these students.

Sorry to say, I find that many students feel just this way. They believe that nothing important ever happened to the members of their families.

But they are wrong!

As you learn more about your families, you will discover interesting, exciting history right in your own families.

You will discover you have family stories, just like this one:

Here we are in a small village in central Europe. It is thousands of miles from this tiny village to Kansas. The year is 1875.

In one of the houses a family sits down to eat their supper. Father, mother and

two children are seated at the table. (Let's pretend that this is your great grandfather's family.)

The father and mother are very tired. They have worked all day in the fields. And there isn't much food on the table. They seem to be very discouraged.

The father speaks. (One thing to remember: Your great grandfather would speak in a foreign language.)

"I'm afraid you children have no future in this country. Your life is going to be very hard. Every day you will go to work in the fields, just as I have done for my whole life. And every night you will go to bed hungry."

Mother then speaks.

"What shall we do, Papa? I want our children to go to school. I want them to have an education. I want our boy to own his own land. I want our girl to have a fine home. I want them to have a wonderful future!"

Father thinks for a moment, then he says, "Mama, today, down at the village, I met a man from America. He said that he worked for the Santa Fe Railroad. He said it was his job to help people like us to go to America and get land in a place he called Kansas. Mama, I've thought carefully about this, and I think we should follow this man's advice. I think we should go to America. Perhaps we can get some land in Kansas, too!"

The children jump up from their chairs. As they dance around the room they cry out, "Where is America? How do we get there? What else can you tell us about our new home in Kansas? When do we leave?"

As you discover the story of your family, you are going to find many stories like this one. Exciting and important things happened to the people in your family.

Listen very carefully. The part of history which tells the story of you and your family has a special name.

It is called your **HERITAGE.**

HERITAGE

That is a very important word.

HERITAGE is your very own history. It is the story of you and your family.

As you study history in school, you will find a part of your **HERITAGE** on just about every page of your history book.

An exciting way to study history is by discovering the story of your own family. You will find that you have many interesting **ancestors**.

Who are **ancestors**?

Your ancestors are the men and women who lived before you were born.

Among your ancestors you will find many pioneers. These pioneers are the people who prepared the way for you.

Chapter Four:
Looking for Your Heritage

"**Heritage** *is a very important word. Right? Heritage is your very own history. It is the story of you and your family."*

Let's think of some of the ways we can discover our heritage.

Is there someone in your family who is interested in **genealogy**? If there is, that person can help you discover the story of your family.

A person who is interested in **genealogy** studies the history of his or her family. A genealogist finds the names of every member of the family going back over many, many years. A genealogist finds out when and where each person was born—all sorts of interesting things like that.

Perhaps someone has written a genealogy book about your family. If your family has such a book, you are really lucky. It will help you learn about your family.

Many of us don't know much about our genealogy. We don't have books written about our families.

But we can discover the story of our familes in other ways—and we can have fun doing it.

First of all, you can look around your house for "pieces" of your heritage. What is a "piece" of heritage?

A piece of old furniture that belonged to one of your ancestors is an interesting "piece" of heritage. So is the crib you used when you were a baby!

Old letters written by someone in your family are really valuable "pieces" of heritage.

A trunk filled with clothing that some persons in your family wore years ago is a wonderful "piece" of heritage.

Look through your house for "pieces" of heritage. Dig into closets and drawers. Keep looking and you will find exciting "pieces" of heritage that tell you about your family.

Old family photographs are just about the most interesting "pieces" of heritage you can find. Family photographs are very valuable. Photographs show you what your ancestors looked like. They show you how they lived and how they dressed.

Study carefully the family photographs you find. Ask your parents to help you answer the following questions:

1. Who are the people in the photograph?
2. Where was the photograph taken?
3. When was the photograph taken?
4. Why was the photograph taken?

"Photographs help you discover your heritage. Old photographs tell you a great deal about your family pioneers!"

The man leaning on the washing machine at the right is my father. This is the hardware store my father owned in Neillsville, Wisconsin. I was born in the house across the street from the hardware store. This picture was taken in 1930.

Chapter Five:
Listening for Your Heritage

You can discover your heritage by listening.

All of us have had wonderful listening experiences. There was the time we listened to our grandfather tell about his first ride in an automobile.

And there was the time our aunt talked about going to a one room country school, "back in the good old days."

Yes, we can learn about our heritage by listening to our parents, grandparents and other adults.

What are the ways we can go about listening for our heritage?

One way is by asking your parents to answer some questions. Say to your parents, "Dad and Mom, I want to learn about what you were doing when you were my age. Would you please answer some questions for me, please?"

Here are some questions to ask your mother and father.

1. When you were my age, where were you living?
2. Tell me about your family. How many brothers and sisters did you have?
3. When you were my age, what did you and your brothers and sisters do for fun?
4. Tell me about your father and mother.
5. What kind of work did your father do?
6. What is something special you remember about your mother?
7. Who were your best friends? Why did you like them?
8. Tell me about your school. What was it like?
9. Do you remember any of your teachers? What were your teachers like? Who was your favorite teacher?
10. What did you like best about school? (And don't say recess!)

11. What did you do for fun when you were my age?
12. Do you remember the best time you had with your family? What did you do?
13. Who was your favorite relative? Tell me about this relative.
14. Did you ever get into trouble with your parents? If you don't mind, please tell me about that time.
15. When you were my age, did you ever think about what you wanted to do when you grew up? What did you think you wanted to be when you grew up?

After listening to your parents answer these questions—and any other questions you can think of—you will know some interesting things about your parents.

Here is a good idea!

Why not ask your grandparents the same questions? And there may be other members of your family, such as aunts and uncles, you can ask these questions.

It is fun listening to people talk about their pasts.

I'm sure you will find many other adults you will want to listen to. Some will be members of your family. Others will be men and women in your town or in your neighborhood.

Why don't you set up a **PEOPLE BANK**?

A **PEOPLE BANK** is a place where you keep the names of men and women you want to talk with. It can be a sheet of paper in your notebook. It can be a box on your desk. Or it can be a bulletin board in your classroom.

You put the names of interesting people in your **PEOPLE BANK**; and as you have time, you go to talk with them.

You will probably put many, many names in your **PEOPLE BANK**. It may take you a long time to talk to all of the people. That is all right. Don't be in a hurry.

Some of the people you may want to visit several times. All of the people you listen to will become your good friends, and they won't mind your coming back for several visits.

It is fun to listen to men and women tell about the past. They can tell you about your heritage and about the pioneers who prepared the way for you.

"Listening . . . is a great way to discover the story of you and your family."

My wife's grandparents, Alvin Ulysses and Viola May Jarrett, after their wedding in 1892. The picture was taken in Holton.

Here is a photograph of my mother's family. My grandfather, Alexander Cameron, is at the right. My mother is the little girl sitting in the old car. This was my grandfather's first automobile. It was made by the International Company. The family was enjoying a Fourth of July picnic in 1910.

UNIT THREE
LISTEN TO THE LAND

Chapter Six:
Voices from the Past

In the summer of 1950 I came to Belleville, Kansas, to play baseball on the Belleville team.

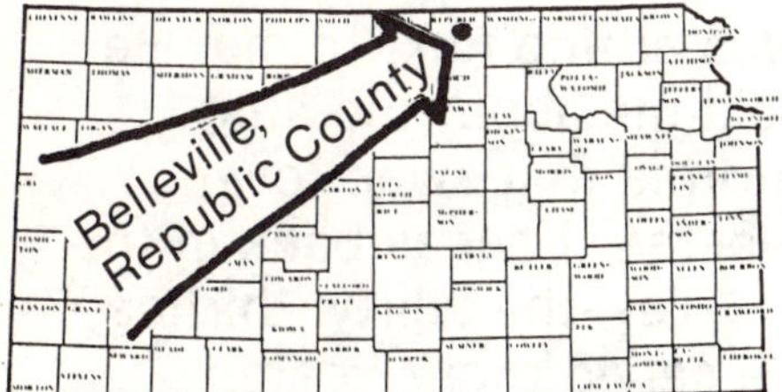

Mr. Royal Henderson, one of the men in town who helped with the baseball team, wanted to show me the country around Belleville.

We climbed into his car and drove out into the farm country. Mr. Henderson knew the story of every farm we passed. He knew the names of the families who had lived on the land. He knew where they came from, and he usually knew what had happened to all the members of the family.

It was fun to listen to Mr. Henderson tell me those interesting stories about the people who lived in Republic County.

Mr. Henderson was just one Kansan who helped me learn to "listen to the land."

Then I met Mr. Merle Nevins who is a rancher in Logan County.

I drove to his ranch in the valley of the Smoky Hill River. I'm glad I went to see him, for he had wonderful stories to tell me.

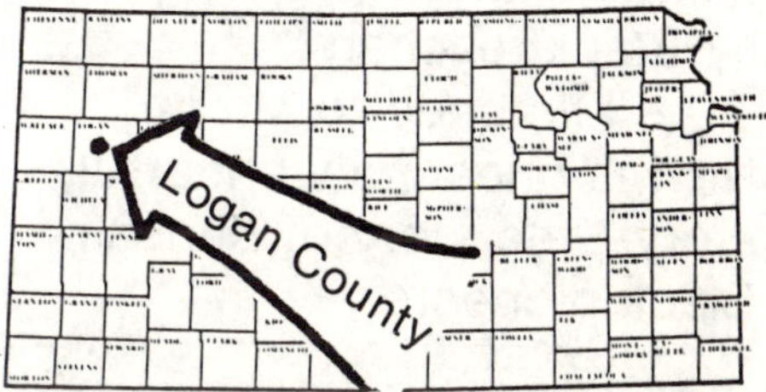

Mr. Nevins is the descendant of Black pioneers who settled in Kansas many years ago.

His ancestors had been slaves in the South. During the Civil War all the slaves were freed; and after that terrible war, many Black families decided to come to Kansas. They wanted to own their own land. They wanted their children to have a future. Mr. Nevin's grandfather and grandmother were among the Black people who made the long, hard trip to Kansas.

Mr. Nevins showed me the place where his grandfather made a dugout in the side of a hill. He told me how his grandfather gathered food from the prairie—wild onions, wild berries, and plums—and how he shot prairie chickens and rabbits.

From Mr. Nevin's ranch we could see three abandoned school houses. Mr. Nevins remembers the time when these schools were filled with Black children, who were taught by Black teachers.

As I listened to Mr. Nevins I heard a wonderful story—the story of Kansas' Black pioneers.

Not long ago I was driving through western Kansas. I stopped in Sharon Springs to have lunch.

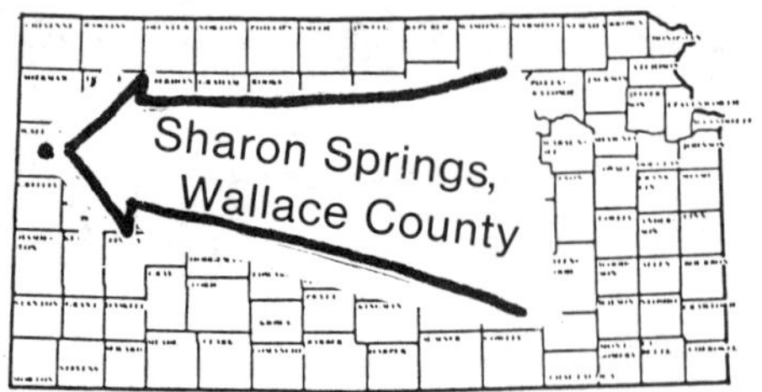

While sitting at the lunch counter, I started to talk with a friendly farmer who was sitting next to me. He told me about the dust storms that swept over western Kansas back in the 1930's—the "dirty 'thirties," he called those years.

He said he remembered the day the first dust storm rolled over the prairie. It was the middle of the day, and it seemed as though the sun had dropped behind a dense black cloud.

His father sent him and his brothers and sisters in to the house. He told them to close all the windows.

Then his father and mother picked up blankets and sheets, soaked them in water, and hurriedly hung the wet blankets and sheets over the windows.

Then the family stood on the front porch . . . and waited . . . and watched.

Suddenly the wind began to blow. The dust came swirling over the ground.

The family dashed into the house and slammed the door. The wind howled outside, and the dust came in through every crack in the house. It was hard to breathe. The rug was covered with almost an inch of fine dust.

This farmer remembered watching his mother as she sat in her rocking chair, quietly praying as the house shook and shuddered in the terrible wind.

And he remembered his father who was sitting in a chair. His father's face was white with anger. He was thinking about the crops in the field that the wind and dust were destroying.

Finally, the dust storm passed. Crops were ruined. Dust was piled on the land in drifts—black snow, the farmers in western Kansas called the dust.

Many families left the land. But this man's family stayed on the land. They worked hard, and today they are proud of their farm.

The man turned to me and said, "You know, Bob, I'm glad that my dad saw the future in this country. Well, got to go now. I've got chores to do. If you are ever in this country again, stop out to see us. So long."

One day I was driving my car along a road in Lyon County. All of a sudden I noticed a cemetery on the east side of the road. I pulled into the cemetery to have a look. (My family will tell you that I don't pass many cemeteries. I usually stop to look.)

I got out of my car and started to walk through the cemeteries. I was in for a surprise—I couldn't read the writing on most of the headstones.

Here is one of the stones I saw. See if you can read it!

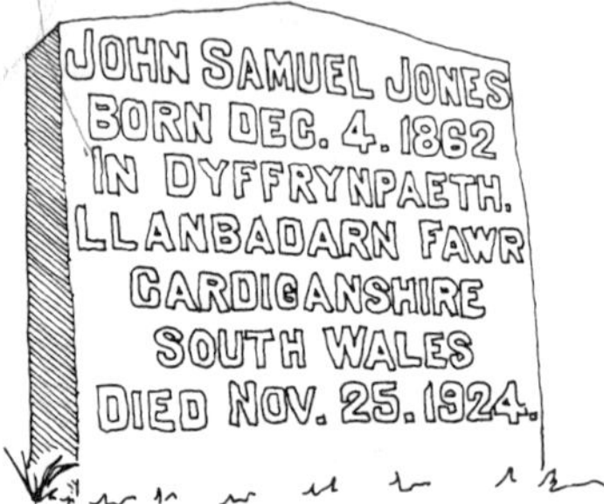

Only if you understand Welsh will you be able to read some of the words on the stone.

Many of the people buried in this cemetery came from Wales, a part of the British Isles.

All of a sudden, another car turned into the cemetery. The driver parked behind my car, got out and walked up to me.

"Interested in our cemetery, are you?" she asked.

"Yes, I am," I replied. And then for the next hour this friendly woman, whose father, mother, grandfather and grandmother were buried in the cemetery, told me stories of these interesting people who came to Kansas from Wales.

Stories such as these show us how important it is to "listen to the land."

I know that the land can't talk, but the men and women who have lived on the land can tell us exciting stories about the pioneers who came to Kansas.

"Kansans are friendly people. They enjoy telling you stories about the pioneers."

"And you will discover that no matter where you live in Kansas, you will find people who can tell you wonderful stories about the pioneers and the land."

The history books you read in school will teach you many things about Kansas.

But the stories you hear from persons such as Mr. Henderson and Mr. Nevins, from farmers in western Kansas and men and women whom you meet in old cemeteries—these stories will help you learn about Kansas, too.

So, why don't you get busy and find men and women who can help you "listen to the land."

Put their names in your **PEOPLE BANK**. I know you'll find many, many men and women who will gladly share with you their memories of the past.

"The stories of the pioneers are all around you in Kansas. You can hear these marvelous stories if you "listen to the land."

HERITAGE SPECIAL

An exciting way to discover the story of the land is by learning about the names which you find on the land. Here are some examples:

Topeka, the capital city of Kansas, is said to be an Indian word meaning "potatoes," or a "place to dig potatoes."

Goessel, a town in Marion county, is named for a sea captain whose vessel brought Mennonite families across the Atlantic Ocean. It is said that the captain died when his vessel sunk during its return trip to Europe.

Rooks County is named for John C. Rooks, a private soldier in the Eleventh Kansas Cavalry during the Civil War. He was killed in action during the war.

Denmark in Lincoln County is named for the country in Europe from which many of the settlers came.

Lyon County in eastern Kansas is named for a general who served in the Union Army during the Civil War. While leading his soldiers against a Confederate army in Missouri, General Lyon was killed. Most of his soldiers were from Iowa and Kansas.

Look around where you live. See what interesting names on the land you can find.

Ask your teacher if you can set up a bulletin board in your classroom on which you can put the interesting names you find.

"There are wonderful stories to be found in the names on the land of Kansas."

Chapter Seven:
A Look at the Land

I want you to pretend that it is a warm, bright, June day. We are standing in a field just outside the town of Elkhart.

Look on the map. Can you find Elkhart?

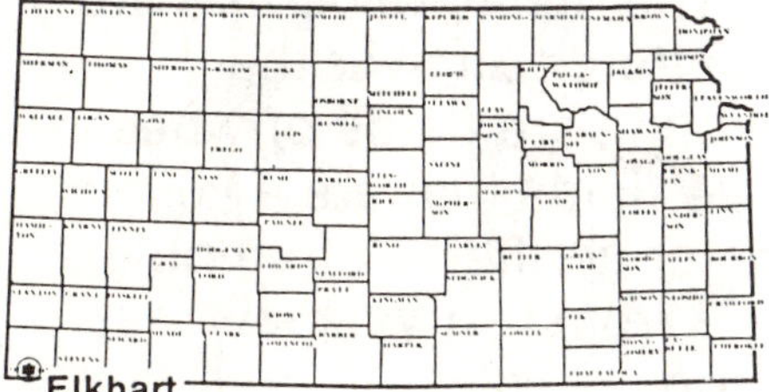

Look across the field. Do you see the big balloon anchored to the ground? And do you see the big basket attached to the bottom of the balloon?

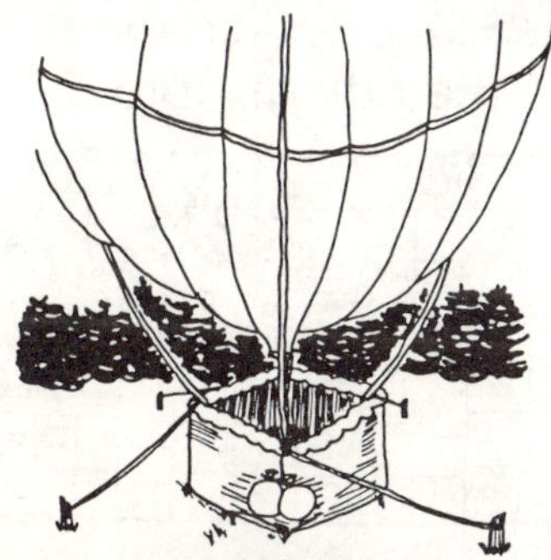

You and I are going to fly across Kansas in that big balloon! Sounds exciting, doesn't it?

Are you ready to go? Got your map? How about the binoculars? Are you dressed warmly? Even though it is warm on the ground, up in the air it will be chilly.

O.K. Everybody into the basket and let's take off!

As we rise into the air look around. You can see the huge sprinkler systems spraying water over the thirsty plants.

And do you see the gas wells sticking up from the ground? Yes, there are hundreds of natural gas wells in this part of Kansas. Look to the east. See the town of Hugoton? Around Hugoton there are large plants where the gas is processed and pumped in underground pipes to homes and factories all over Kansas and the West.

The soft breeze out of the south gently pushes our balloon through the clear sky.

Except for irrigated fields, the land below us looks very dry. The grass and other vegetation look brown. And there aren't many trees at all.

What's that below us? Looks like a bunch of trees growing in a long row!

That's the Arkansas River. The trees grow along the river. You don't see water in the river because much of the year it is dry.

The Arkansas isn't much of a river now, but in pioneer days fur traders, explorers, and covered wagon pioneers followed the river. A branch of the Santa Fe trail went along the north side of that famous river.

Let's check our map and see where we are.

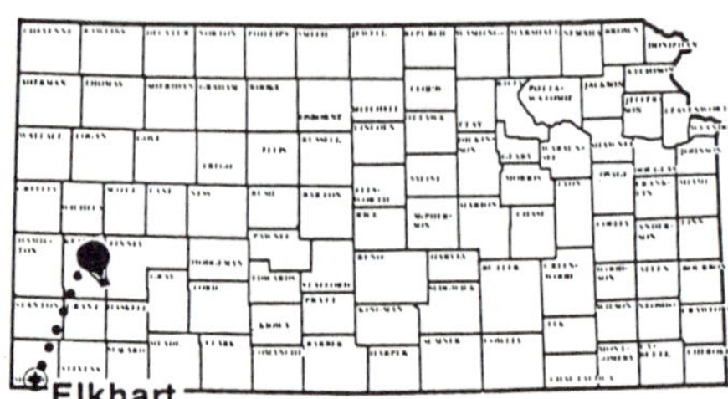

Here is where we are—we are over Kearny County.

The wind seems to be stronger now, doesn't it. We are making good time. Our path is just about straight north.

Quick—look down! See, there's another river. This is the Smoky Hill River. Can you imagine seeing the stage coaches rolling along the old Smoky Hill Trail? Over there a little ways is Mr. Nevins' ranch. Do you remember my telling you about Mr. Nevins and his pioneer family?

The green fields that are scattered all over the ground are fields of wheat. The fields that are a yellow color are fields of stubble left from last year's wheat crop.

We are now passing over some of the finest wheat country in the world!

Let's check our map so we don't get lost. O.K. Here we are . . . right over Thomas County. And over there is the city of Colby.

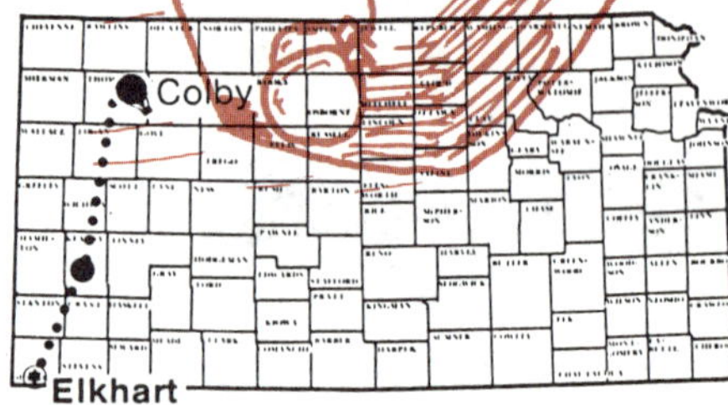

Hang on, everybody! The wind is shifting. Hold on!

The big balloon gives a lurch and leans toward the east. The wind is now directly out of the west, and we are sailing along above interstate highway—I-70.

Just think! Not many years ago covered wagons crawled over the Kansas plains. And today automobiles and trucks whiz over the ribbons of concrete.

The land is mostly dry-looking and the vegetation is brown. There are a few small towns and farms and ranches. Once in a while we see an oil field, where the big pumps work up and down, pumping the precious "black gold" from deep under the ground.

Where are we now? Let's check the map. We are passing over Rooks County.

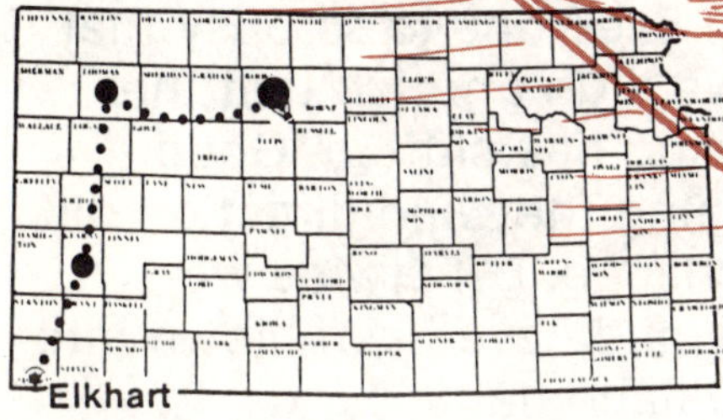

All of a sudden the wind shifts again. Our balloon changes direction and we are scooting along to the southeast quietly and swiftly.

Don't any of you sleep. There is a lot of Kansas yet to be seen.

Look down! There is Hays, Kansas. And to the east of Hays is Victoria. See the twin spires of the great church rising in the air? They call that church "The Cathedral of the Plains." It was built by German-Russian pioneers who came to Ellis County so they could have their own land and be free to follow their religion.

Silently we slide through the air. The wind whispers about the ropes that hold the basket to the balloon.

Time to look over the side of the basket because we are passing over Great Bend.

See how the Arkansas River makes a big turn here—makes a great bend—and that's how the city got its name!

Just think! We are now over the land that was visited by Spanish explorers and priests more than three hundred years ago. Can you imagine what these Spanish thought about the land?

And if you look carefully, you can see traces of the Santa Fe trail on the land. Hundreds of heavy freight wagons passed along the trail, and the ruts they wore remain in the prairie.

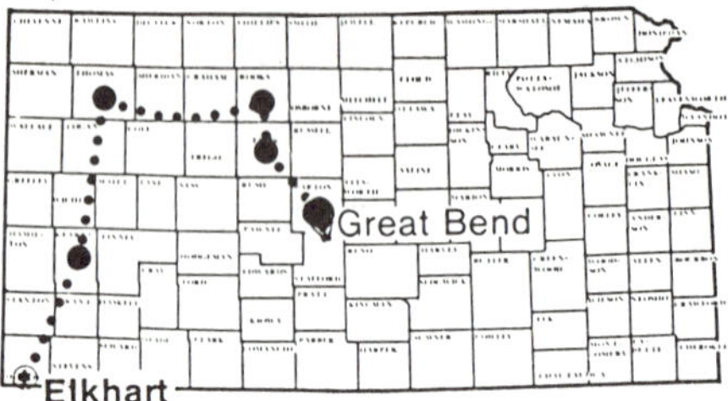

Our balloon is now passing over farm and ranch land. The land is very level, and we see a town here and there.

Look up ahead! What in the world is that? Looks as though there are millions of tiny mirrors shining up from the ground! And notice how red the earth has become!

We are looking at one of the most beautiful parts of Kansas. Those are the Red Hills of southern Kansas. The ground and hills are covered with bits of a mineral called mica, which is just like glass. So we see the mica twinkling brightly in the sun.

Can you imagine the land below us covered with herds of buffalo? And can you see bands of Indians chasing the huge beasts? Can you see the Indian camps, with their tipis and smoke from their cooking fires rising in the air?

The Indians loved this land, and for years the Indians and the white pioneers fought for control of the land. That city over there is Medicine Lodge, and a treaty between the Indians and the white settlers was signed near the town in 1867. You'll want to visit Medicine Lodge some day and see the famous monument that tells us about the treaty.

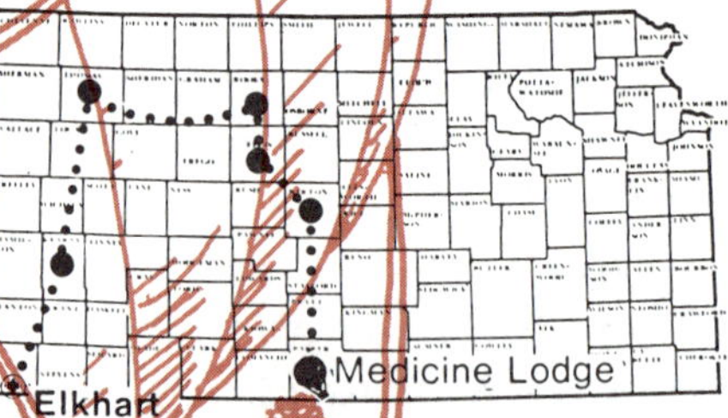

Everyone is so busy that we didn't notice that the wind has shifted. Good thing the wind direction did change. Otherwise we would have been blown into Oklahoma!

Our balloon is racing just about northeast now.

That's the city of Wichita ahead of us. See the interstate highway coming up from the south. That highway passes over the same ground that the cattle trails passed over, more than a hundred years ago.

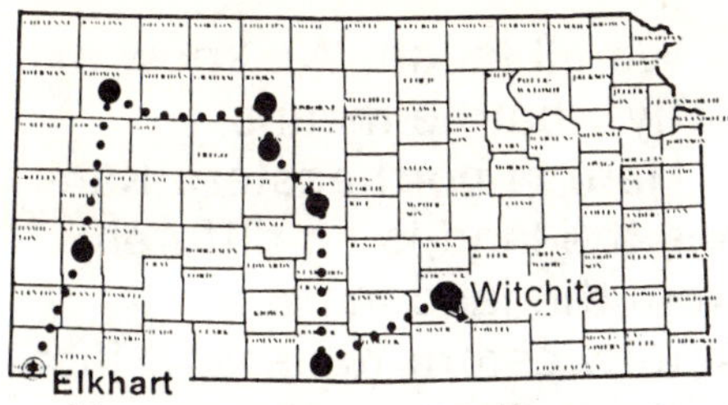

Now we are over the cattle country of Butler County. See the herds of cattle quietly grazing on the grass? And there are many oil wells to look at also.

Our balloon swings a little more to the north, and we head directly over the Kansas "Flint Hills." Aren't they beautiful? Just look at those hills! Don't they look like grass-covered ocean waves?

This is some of the finest cattle country in the world. And it is easy to see why. The grass is bright green—looks good enough to eat, doesn't it? Well, the cows certainly think so!

Why are they called the Flint Hills? Well, because bits of hard stone, or flint, are found lying on the ground. The Indians used these pieces of flint for their tools and weapons. So, that's why they are called the Flint Hills.

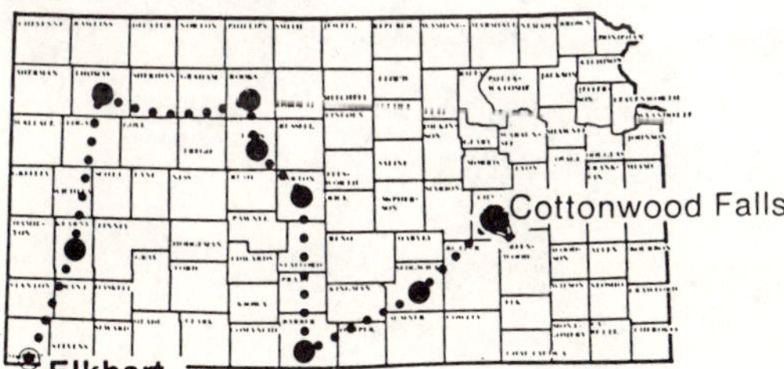

Look below! We are over Chase County, and I want you to see the courthouse that stands in Cottonwood Falls. It is one of the most beautiful courthouses in Kansas.

How the land has changed! Do you notice the change? In western Kansas the land, which is not irrigated, looks brown and dry. The land which is slipping beneath us now is green and bright.

To the east we can see Emporia, and just south of Emporia is the Welsh cemetery which I visited.

We are really making good time now. Up ahead we see Topeka, the capital of the State of Kansas. We pass over the interstate highway again. Look how hilly the land has become, and patches of woods cover much of the ground.

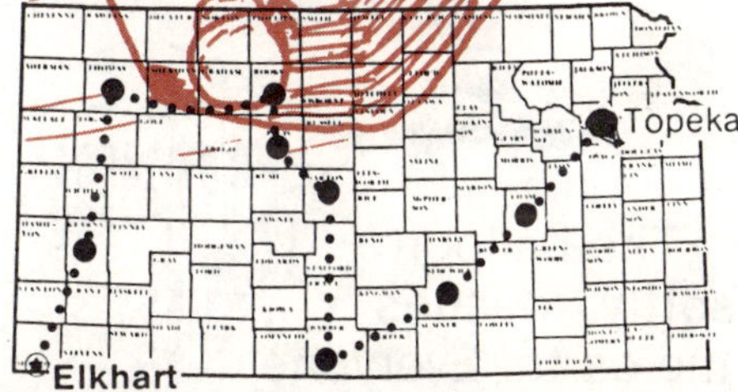

Now, look to the east! You can see Kansas City, Kansas, and its neighbor, Kansas City, Missouri.

A couple of minutes more and we'll see the Missouri River. Yes, there it is! See that huge river shining in the sun?

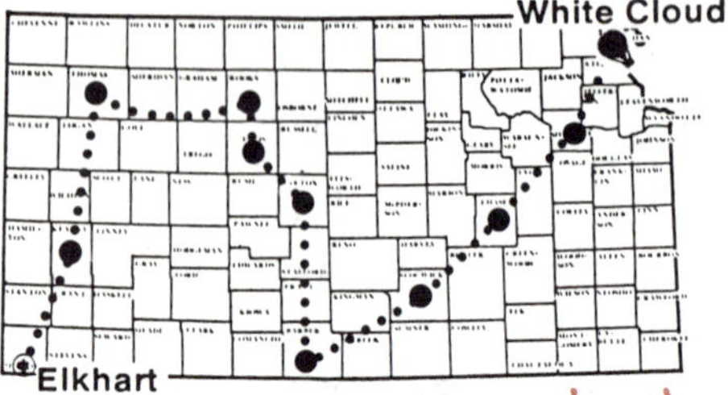

The Missouri River comes closer and closer. Down there—that's the spot we want to land. That's the town of White Cloud, once a booming, prosperous town, back in the 1850's, back in the days when Kansas was very young. Today White Cloud is just a quiet little river town.

I'll bet the folks in White Cloud will be surprised to have a balloon drop in on them!

The balloon softly touches the earth. Everyone is glad to have the earth underfoot again.

One of the boys says, "Are you sure we are still in Kansas?"

We all laugh. We know exactly what he means.

Here in northeastern Kansas the land is so different from the land in southwestern Kansas. It just doesn't seem as though we could still be in the same state.

Our balloon ride over Kansas was a lot of fun, wasn't it? And we had a chance to learn some very important things about Kansas.

1. We learned that Kansas is a very large State. Even with brisk winds pushing our balloon along, it took us a long time to cross Kansas.

2. We learned that there are many different parts to Kansas. There are the green tree-covered hills along the Missouri River.

There are the rolling, grass-covered Flint Hills. In northwestern Kansas there are huge wheat fields. And we saw thousands of acres of land in southwestern Kansas that was irrigated.

And we saw the barren western prairies, which are covered with cacti and bunch grass.

Chapter Eight:
Rain, Wind and Sun

In the last chapter we learned that Kansas is made up of many different kinds of land.

Eastern Kansas has many trees, green, grass-covered hills and rich farm land.

As we floated over western Kansas we saw a different land. Most of western Kansas is prairie country. There are few trees, and except for the irrigated fields, the land appears dry and brown.

Let's see if we can discover why the parts of Kansas look so different.

First, let's pick up Kansas from the map and turn the state on its side. Now look at Kansas!

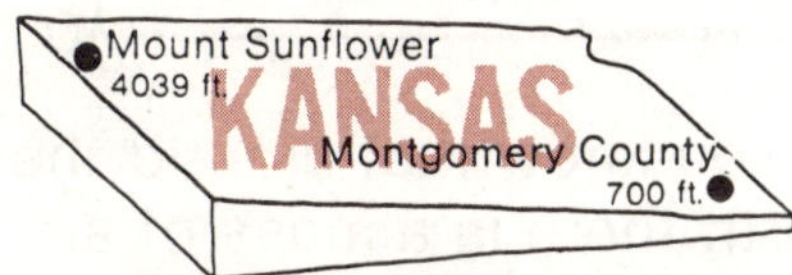

What does the map show us now?

It shows us that Kansas runs uphill from east to west. Do you see that?

Students who live in Wallace County climb to the top of Mount Sunflower, and they are standing on land which is 4,039 feet above sea level. This is the highest spot in Kansas.

On the other hand, students who live in Montgomery county in southeastern Kansas are on land which is 700 feet above sea level.

So, as we travel across Kansas, going from east to west, we go steadily uphill.

Here is the important fact!

As the land becomes higher it also becomes drier. Western Kansas has much less rainfall than eastern Kansas. That is why the land and vegetation of western Kansas is so different from the land and vegetation we find in eastern Kansas.

The amount of rainfall that falls upon the land makes the difference between the eastern and western parts of Kansas.

How many of you know what a rain gauge is? Here is a drawing of a rain gauge.

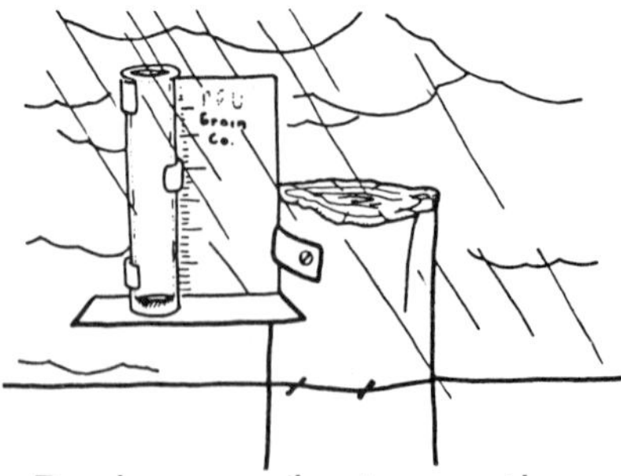

During a rainstorm, the rain gauge catches rain water. After the storm has passed, you can look at the gauge and know how much rain fell during the storm.

I'm sure you have all heard your dad say, "We had an inch of rain last night." And TV weatherpersons are always talking about the amounts of rain that fell in different parts of Kansas.

Look at the map below. This is what is known as a rainfall map of Kansas.

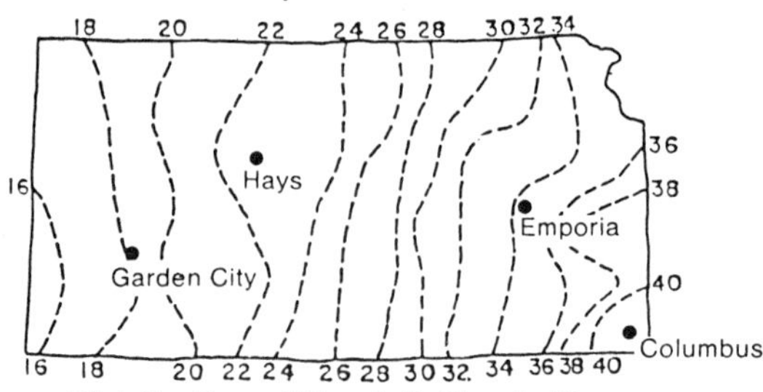

Distribution of Precipitation in Kansas

Let me explain the map.

If you live near Columbus, in the southeastern corner of Kansas, you will receive about 40 inches of rainfall during the year.

Near Emporia between 34 and 36 inches of rain falls in a year.

Now look farther west. If you live at Hays you will get between 22 and 24 inches of rainfall in a year's time.

Those of you who live near Garden City will receive between 20 and 18 inches of rain.

Look at the map and find where you live. How much rain usually falls on your land?

Why is there less rainfall in western Kansas than in eastern Kansas? That is a good question. Let's find the answer.

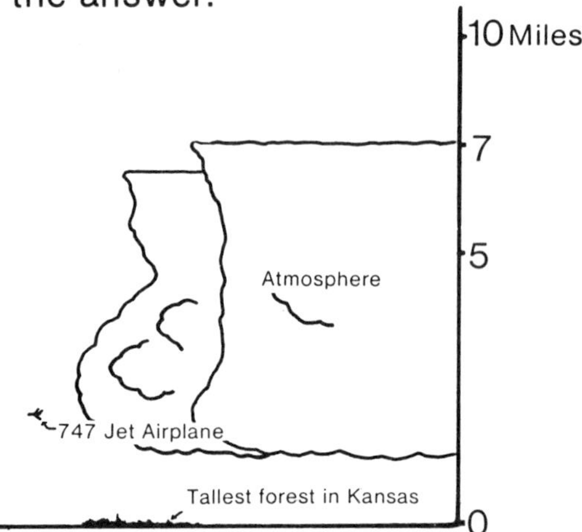

You know that around the Earth there is a mass of air. It is called the atmosphere.

This mass of air, or atmosphere, does not stay in one place. It is constantly moving.

For example, the mass of air moves from west to east across the United States and Kansas.

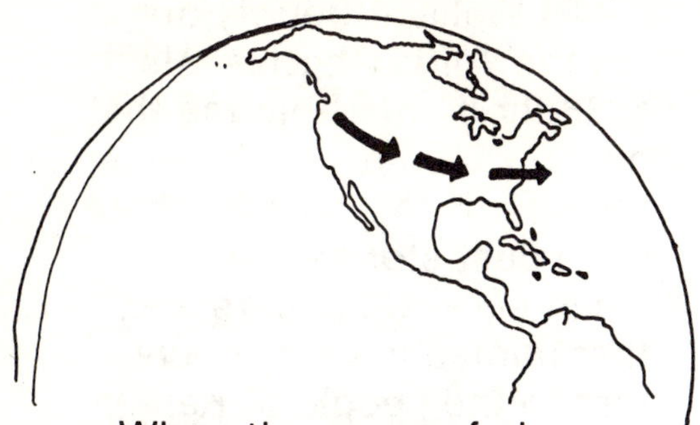

When the mass of air comes in from the Pacific Ocean, it is carrying huge quantities of moisture. This moisture, of course, was picked up from the ocean.

Then the mass of moving air strikes the mountains in the western part of our country. The air mass rises higher and higher. As the air becomes cool, it drops the moisture it has been carrying. Rain or snow falls on the mountains.

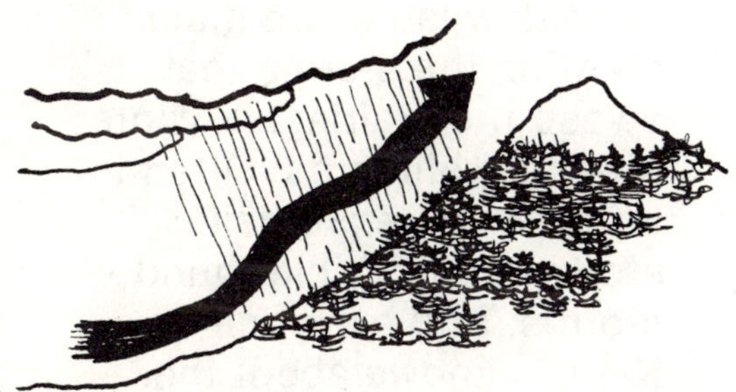

So, as the mass of air crosses the western mountains, it loses most of the moisture. When the air comes over western Kansas it is very dry. Very little rain falls.

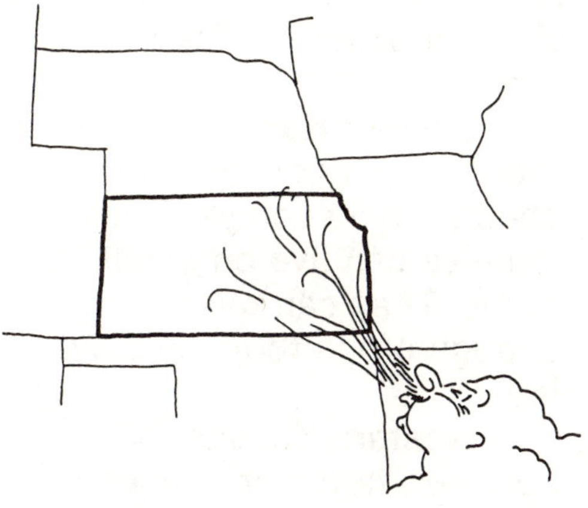

Currents of air from the Gulf of Mexico, however, carry moisture north. By the time these currents reach central and eastern Kansas, they have picked up a great deal of moisture. As they pass over the land, the moisture falls to the ground as rain. This means that there is more rainfall in eastern Kansas than there is in the western part of the state.

Why is rainfall so important to Kansas?

I'm sure you all know the answer to that question. It is because Kansas is a farming and ranching state. Farmers and ranchers need rainfall in order to raise their crops and to feed their livestock.

In eastern Kansas, where there is thirty or forty inches of rain each year, families can live on small farms. They can raise enough crops to make a living.

In western Kansas, however, farms and ranches must be very large. With less rainfall, the land produces fewer crops. So farms and ranches must be large in order to produce the crops needed to support the farmer and his family.

There is one other problem with Kansas' rainfall. The rainfall map shows us the amount of rain that **usually** falls.

But as every Kansan knows, there can be more or less rainfall in a year. More often than not there are periods of drought—years in which less than the usual, or normal, amount of rain falls.

Remember the man I met in the restaurant in Sharon Springs? He told me about life in Wallace County during the "dirty 'thirties." In 1936 the farmer told me that only six inches of rain fell in the county. No wonder there were dust storms.

I'm sure you understand that rainfall is very important to the people of Kansas. And you can also understand why farmers and ranchers in western Kansas are interested in irrigation.

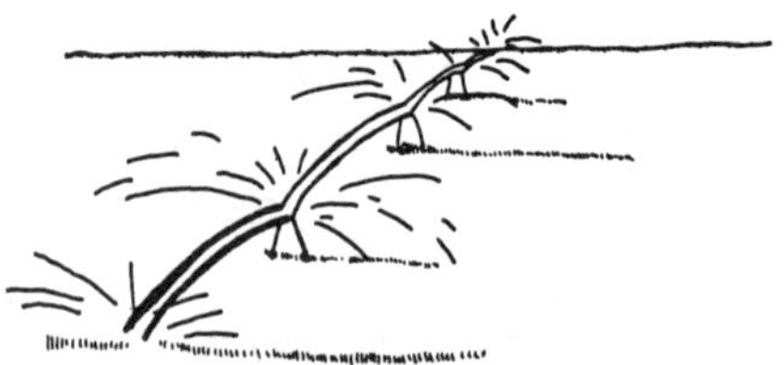

Rainfall is only one part of the weather picture in Kansas. You know that, don't you?

When we talk about the Kansas weather we must mention the storms that sweep the prairies. In winter there are blizzards. Often in summer there are hail storms and terrible thunder storms. And everyone in Kansas knows about the fierce tornadoes that roar over the land. It was in Kansas, you know, that a young farm girl by the name of Dorothy, was whisked away by a tornado and deposited in the Land of Oz. Right?

And every Kansan knows that winters can be terribly cold, with temperatures plunging to many degrees below zero.

Then comes summer, and the temperatures can soar to well above 100 degrees.

When the pioneers came to Kansas they had to learn to live with this weather. What do you suppose the pioneers thought about the blizzards? What do you suppose they thought about the hot, dry summers?

Yes, they had to fight the rain, the wind, and the sun. We know that many pioneers gave up and left Kansas. The weather drove them out.

Those who stayed on the land and in the towns prepared the way for you and your families.

Chapter Nine:
The First Kansans

As you "listen to the land" you will hear many interesting stories about Kansas. For example, as you walk among the beautiful Kansas Pyramids in Gove County you might find stories that took place thousands of years ago!

Watch the ground carefully! You might find a strange looking stone—like this one:

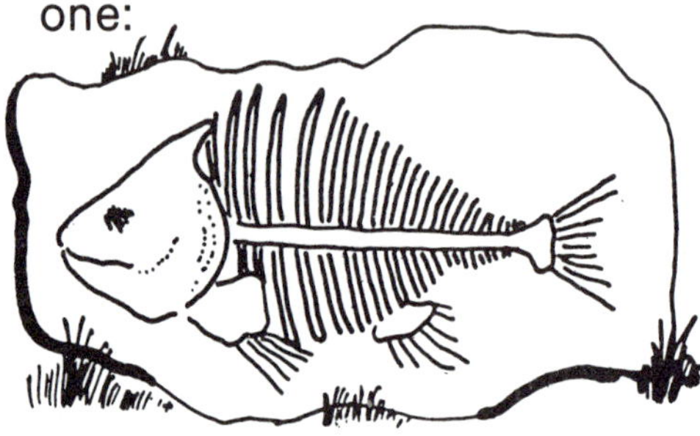

What do you see in this rock? Yes, there is a clear picture of a fish.

You know what this kind of stone picture is called, don't you? It is a **fossil**.

Here is another fossil.

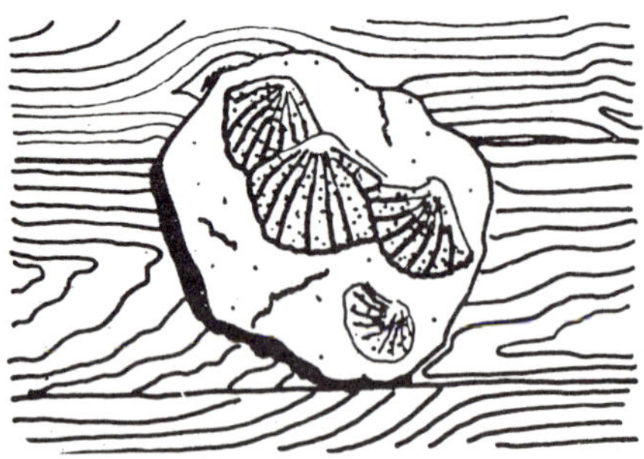

My family and I found a fossil like this one in the park at Wilson Lake in central Kansas.

Scientists who are known as **paleontologists** can tell us about these fossils. The fossils show us that Kansas was once a very different land than what it is today.

The fossil fish and fossil shells tell us that centuries ago a huge ocean covered much of what is now Kansas.

As the animals who lived in the ocean died, they sank to the bottom of the sea. The dead creatures were covered by layers of mud.

Thousands of years passed, and the mud turned to stone. The outlines of the ancient fish and shells remained in the rock.

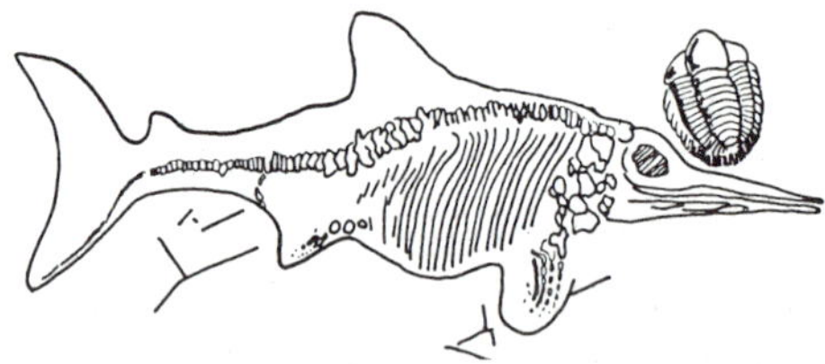

Fossils of all shapes and sizes are found in almost every part of Kansas. Huge fossil turtles, fossils of flying reptiles and the fossil remains of tiny animals that look like horses have been found buried in the ground.

Go to your People Bank. See if you have the names of men and women in your community who collect fossils. Ask these people to come to your class and to show you their collections of fossils.

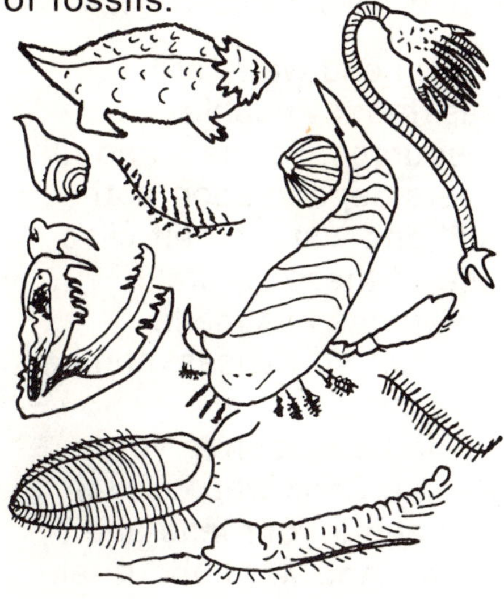

I want you to meet another scientist—the **geologist.**

A geologist is a scientist who studies the history of the rocks that make up our Earth.

Geologists want to know about the layers of rock and gravel that lie under the ground.

A geologist can tell us some interesting stories about our land. First, a geologist can tell us about the huge sheet of ice, known as glaciers, that many centuries ago moved down to cover the northeastern part of Kansas.

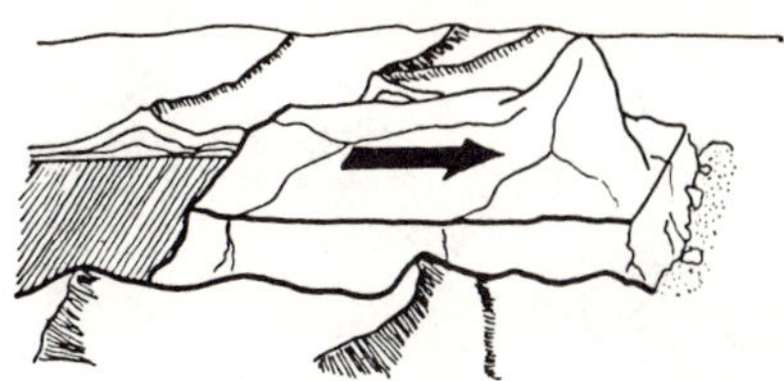

The huge glacier moved slowly across the land. It carved out valleys and piled up rocks and dirt to make hills and ridges.

The glacier had much to do with how the land in the northeastern corner of Kansas looks. Remember when we flew over Kansas in our balloon? We noticed that this part of Kansas was very hilly. The glacier made the land look like that.

The geologist knows that our Earth is made up of layers of rock and gravel. Deep under the ground there are layers of gravel which hold huge quantities of water.

The wells that provide us with drinking water must reach into these layers.

The irrigation wells that we saw as our balloon drifted over southwestern Kansas must also reach down into these layers of water-bearing gravel.

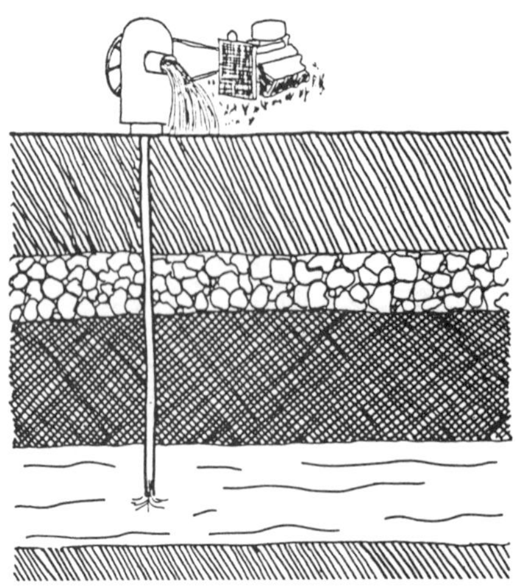

In some parts of Kansas geologists have found oil and natural gas locked up in these rock layers. These pockets of oil and gas may be thousands of feet under the ground. It takes hard work and a great deal of money to drill the wells that bring this oil and gas to the surface.

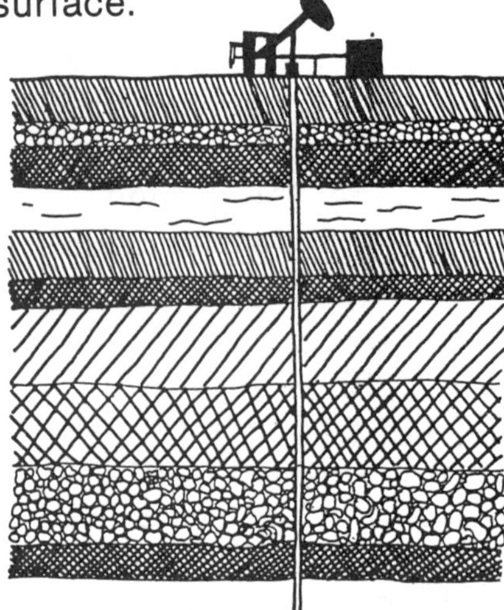

You can see that the geologist helps us understand the history of our land. They know the story of the layers of rock that make up the Earth.

But the most valuable part of our Kansas land is the soil which lies right on top! It is this soil which produces Kansas' valuable crops.

Soil and water are Kansas' most valuable resources. Farmers and ranchers depend upon both soil and water. Their wise use of these natural resources has made agriculture Kansas' number one industry.

Find a person in your People Bank who can tell you about your land and water. And what about taking a field trip? I know there are many adults in your People Bank who would be glad to show you the land. Perhaps they would also take you on a trip to look for fossils.

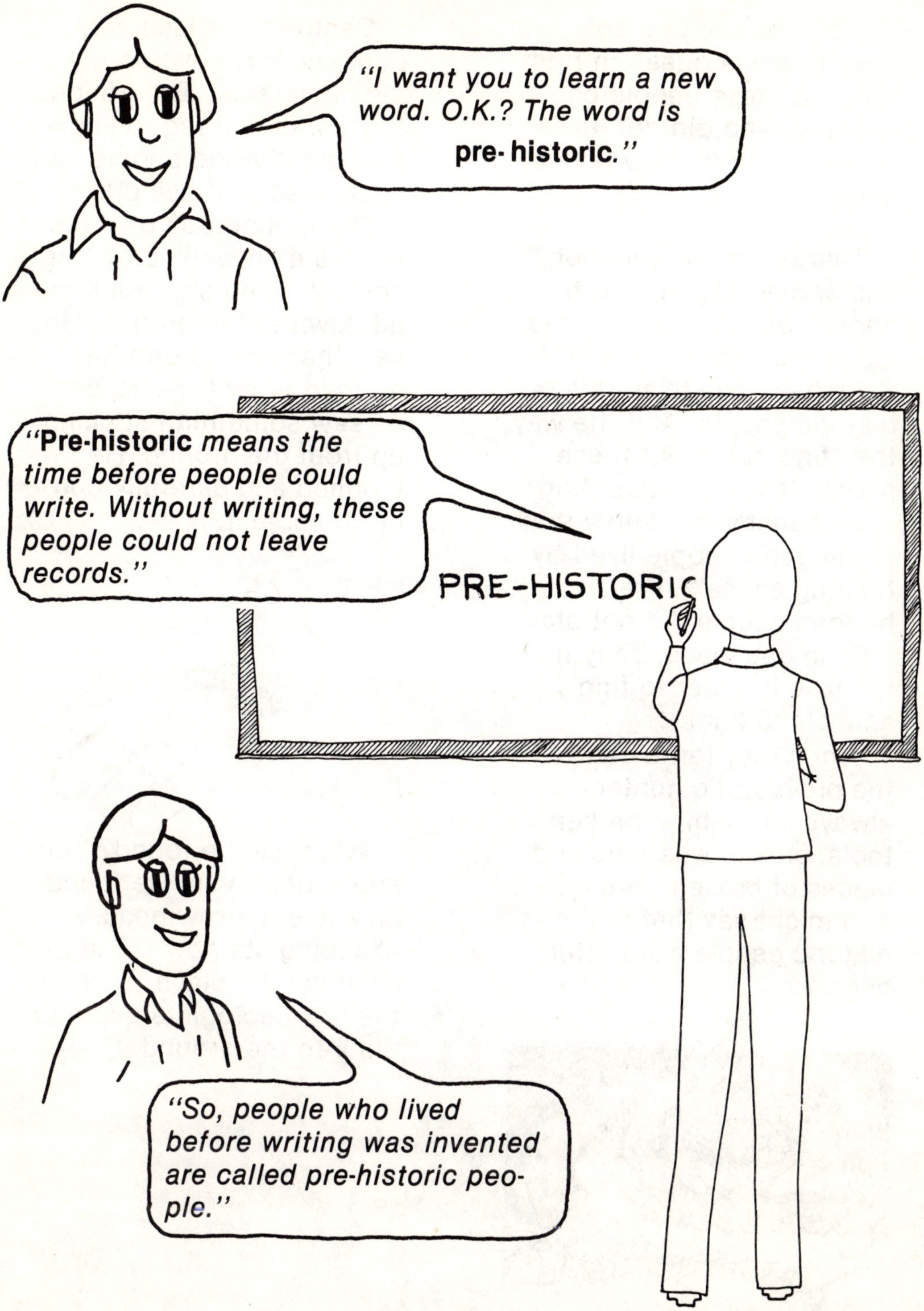

"**Pre-historic** *means the time before people could write. Without writing, these people could not leave records.*"

PRE-HISTORIC

"So, people who lived before writing was invented are called pre-historic people."

Some of you probably want to ask a question right now: "If these people could not write and did not leave written records, how do we know anything about them?"

That is a good question, and **archaeologists** are the people who can answer the question.

Archaeologists study pre-historic people. And the way they find out about these people is really interesting.

Archaeologists know that pre-historic people lived by hunting animals. Pre-historic people did not stay long in one place. They had to move in order to find animals to hunt.

When they left a camp, the pre-historic hunters always left behind broken tools, broken weapons and pieces of broken pottery. You might say that pre-historic people were litter bugs.

Centuries passed and dust and dirt covered the old camp sites. Before long there was nothing to show that pre-historic people had once lived in these places

Then, hundreds of years later, a man walked by this ancient camp site. He looked down at the ground. He saw that a rainstorm had washed away the dirt, and he saw something sticking up from the ground. He stopped and carefully dug up the object.

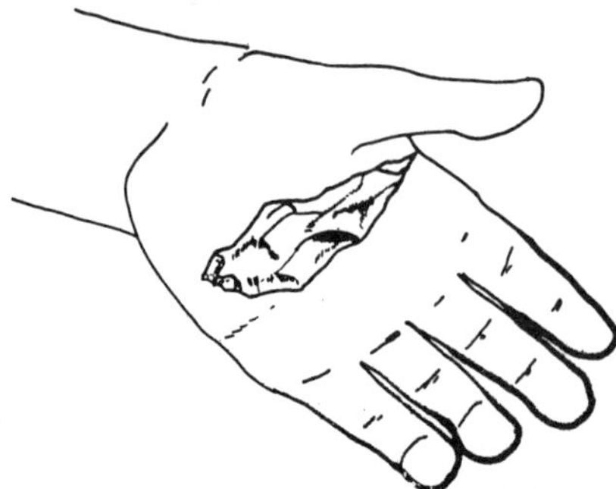

What had he found? You know, don't you. He found an ancient arrow head. Archaeologists now come to examine the place. Carefully the archaeologists begin to dig into the ground.

As they dig away the dirt that covers the ancient camp site,the archeaologists hope to find pottery, tools and weapons left behind by the pre-historic hunters.

Archaeologists must be very careful as they dig. They don't want to overlook even the smallest piece of pottery. Everything they find will help them understand how these pre-historic people lived.

Are there any pre-historic camp sites in your part of Kansas?

Go to your People Bank and find the persons who can tell you about these places. Perhaps you can take a field trip to examine a pre-historic camp site. That would really be exciting.

"Now let's find out how pre-historic people lived."

Pre-historic people lived in small groups or bands. Usually the members of the band came from the same family.

The band camped along streams and rivers where they could get water for drinking and cooking. Women and children picked berries from bushes. They gathered the nuts that fell from the trees, and they looked for plants and roots they could eat.

They lived in huts made from branches and animal skins. In some parts of Kansas they found caves in which to live. A cave made a very good camp site.

Pre-historic people wore clothing made from animal skins. This kind of clothing was neither very warm nor comfortable in the winter. During the warm summer months they probably wore very little clothing.

The camp was a very busy place. Women were preparing food to eat. Some were making clothing from animal skins. It was also the women's job to make pottery out of clay. After making the pots from soft clay, the pots were put in the ashes of the fire to harden.

The men also had work to do. They made tools and weapons out of pieces of wood, stone and bone. This was hard work. It must have taken many, many hours to chip an arrow head or a spear point out of a piece of stone.

With their crude weapons in their hands, the men left camp to hunt. Only skillful—and very lucky—hunters brought back meat. Most of the time the hunters returned without having killed any animals.

Once in a while the hunters were able to drive a herd of wild animals, such as buffalo, over a steep cliff. Dozens of animals would die as a result of falling down the cliff. For a few days the people of the band would have all the meat they could eat.

Life was very, very hard for pre-historic people. They had no medicines to give to their sick children. They had no way to help members of the band recover from injuries.

Their greatest enemy, however, was hunger. In dry years they could not find food. The herds of animals wandered off to find grass and water. And the pre-historic hunters had to leave their camps and follow the animals.

As centuries passed, pre-historic people learned to make better tools and weapons. Some of the men traveled to the place in Kansas we now call the Flint Hills. There they picked up pieces of flint which were used for their arrow heads and spear points.

Even more important, they learned how to plant seeds and how to raise crops of food. After they learned how to farm, the pre-historic people did not have to spend all their time hunting.

They now had time to build better houses in which to live. Their houses were usually made of tree limbs and dirt. Wooden posts held up the roofs.

Gradually the people changed the way they lived. They began to have religious ceremonies. Each year at certain times they would hold dances and feasts to honor the god of the rain and the god of the harvest.

The people in the village selected men to be their leaders. The older men of the village taught the boys how to hunt. From the women in the village the girls learned how to care for the crops and how to prepare food and to make clothing.

Nearly every county in Kansas has a pre-historic village or camp site. Check with the people in your People Bank. Perhaps some of them would take you for a visit to one of these pre-historic camp sites!

"Isn't it fun to learn about your heritage? And you discover your heritage by looking and by listening."
"Now I would like you to meet a friend of mine. She is another Kansas pioneer, and her name is Susie Sunflower."
"Hi, students. I'll bet you all know where I got my name, don't you?"
"That's right. I'm named for the beautiful sunflower, the State flower of Kansas."
"Are you ready to learn more about Kansas? O.K. Here is part two of Dr. Manley's book. You are going to read stories about the people who are a part of your Kansas Pioneer Heritage. Listen carefully."

"The American buffalo is the State animal of Kansas. The buffalo is also known as the American bison."

"The sunflower is the State flower of Kansas."

"The cottonwood is the State tree of Kansas. This beautiful tree is often called the "pioneer tree of Kansas." Do you know why?"

"The State bird of Kansas is the western meadow lark."

HERITAGE SPECIAL HERITAGE SPECIAL HERITAGE SPECIAL HERITAGE SPECIAL

UNIT FOUR:
PEOPLE OF THE PLAINS:
INDIANS, EUROPEANS AND AMERICANS

In the next unit you are going to hear some interesting and exciting stories about these PEOPLE OF THE PLAINS.

Chapter Ten:
The Spanish and the French

In the year 1492 Columbus discovered America. The people who lived in Europe were very excited about America. And in the years after Columbus found the New World hundreds of daring men set off for America. The most famous and the most successful of the early explorers came from Spain.

These Spanish built an empire which included Mexico. In 1540 a Spanish officer, Coronado, led an army north from Mexico in search of a rich country where there was supposed to be Seven Cities of Gold. What an army Coronado commanded! There were 200 Spanish horsemen; 70 foot soldiers; 1,000 Indian servants; 1,200 horses and mules; and great herds of cattle, hogs and sheep.

With flags flying and trumpets blasting, the army started out. The Spanish knew that they would find and conquer the Seven Cities of Gold.

Coronado's men on the march

For a year this great army tramped across the deserts and mountains of Mexico and the southwestern part of the United States. Finally they came upon some large Indian villages, known as pueblos. But these Indians did not live in beautiful mansions; and they didn't have any gold or silver.

One day, however, Coronado learned that the Indians had a slave. This slave said he had been captured by the Indians and that his home was in a land far to the north. It was a rich country, whose rulers ate from plates of gold. It was in fact a land of gold. The slave called the land Quivira.

Coronado and his men were convinced that Quivira was the land they sought. It must be the land where lay the Seven Cities of Gold.

With thirty-six Spanish soldiers and several Indian guides, including the slave, Coronado began to trudge northeast, across the great prairie.

The Spanish traveled for forty-two days over the vast grassland. They killed buffalo and usually ate the meat raw. Once in a while they built fires from buffalo chips and cooked the meat.

Coronado's Cross in Ford County

On June 29, 1541, Coronado and his men crossed the Arkansas River, probably near this place shown in the photograph. The priest who was with the Spanish held a thanksgiving celebration, thanking God for a safe journey. Since June 29 was a Catholic holy day, named for St. Peter and St. Paul, the Spanish named the river for these two saints—they called it the St. Peter and St. Paul River.

Finally, Coronado and his Spanish soldiers reached the place which the Indian slave told them was the land of Quivira.

Where were the rich cities? Where was the gold? Where was the silver?

The Spanish saw villages of Indians. They met tall, handsome Indians—Coronado thought some of the men were nearly seven feet tall! But these Indians, who were probably Wichita Indians, were poor. They had neither gold nor silver.

Coronado was angry. He killed the Indian slave who had led him on this wild goose chase. He ordered his men to turn around. They would return to Mexico.

Where was Coronado when he decided to turn around? Historians have argued about that for years. The best guess is that the Spanish were somewhere in central Kansas, perhaps in Rice County.

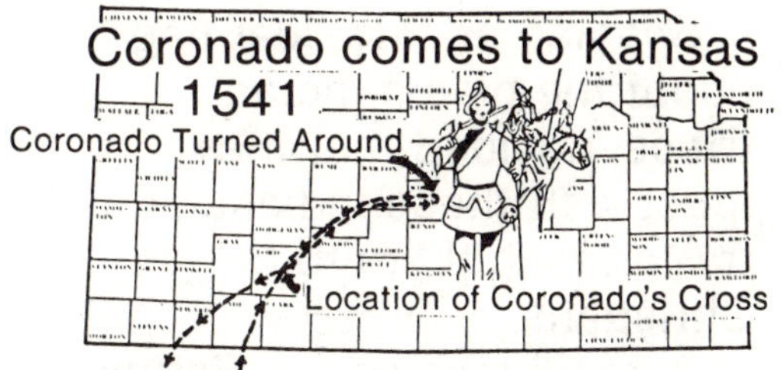

Later Coronado and several other members of his army wrote about their trip into Kansas. They said that the prairie land was very fertile. Coronado said that the country reminded him of Spain. He found nuts, wild grapes and other fruits similar to the nuts and fruits that grew in Spain. Yes, the Spanish agreed that they had seen a wonderful, amazing country. But there was no gold.

Do you suppose Coronado and his Spanish soldiers realized what they had done?

The Coronado expedition is one of the great stories of history. Coronado and his men found a vast new country. The Spanish introduced the horse to the Indians, and in a little while we'll find out just how important the horse was to the Kansas Indians.

And while Coronado did not find gold and silver, he found a good land and he found people living on the land—the Indians.

Spanish priests, learning about the plains Indian tribes, decided that they must visit these Indians and try to teach them to be Christians.

A very brave priest, Father Juan de Padilla, came to live among the Indians of Quivira. But after a very short time among the Indians, Father Padilla was killed by the Indians.

This beautiful cross in Rice County tells the story of Father Juan de Padilla, the brave missionary.

About two hundred years after Coronado made his way across the prairie, French explorers and traders came to Kansas.

They came from Canada and from trading posts along the Mississippi River.

They came to find wealth, too, just as the Spanish had. But the French looked for wealth of another kind. They wanted to trade with the Indians for precious furs.

In the early 1700's French traders visited the Indian villages in eastern Kansas. Then in the year 1724 (how many years was this after Coronado had visited Kansas?) a very famous French explorer and trader, by the name of Bourgmont, visited Kansas.

Bourgmont visits the Indians of Kansas 1724

In these last few pages we have covered hundreds of years of history. Just remember: The Spanish explorer, Coronado, came to Kansas in 1541. In 1724 the French, under Bourgmont, traveled across Kansas.

By the time Bourgmont came to Kansas, this prairie country had become fairly well known. It was no longer a prairie wilderness. The explorers, both Spanish and French, had done their jobs well. They were fine pioneers. They had prepared the way for others.

And what had the explorers learned about the land that one day would be Kansas?

They learned about the great prairie that stretched for hundreds of miles. The Spanish compared the Kansas prairie to an ocean of grass.

They saw great herds of buffalo.

The Spanish brought the horse to the Indians. And they also introduced cattle, hogs, sheep and goats to the people of the New World. None of those animals was here before the Spanish came.

The French learned about the Indians of Kansas. They wanted to trade with the Indians. The Indians, on the other hand, learned that the French had wonderful things to trade. In return for furs, the French gave to the Indians guns and axes, cotton and wool cloth; glass beads and fine glass mirrors; and tin cups and

plates. Everything the French traders showed to the Indians was so very much better than the things the Indians used before the white men came. So the Indians really wanted to trade with the French.

"The Spanish and the French discovered a vast, exciting land."

"The Spanish called the new country Quivira. But one day it would be known as Kansas."

"The European explorers discovered the land . . . and they found interesting people living on the land . . . the Indians."

A VERY SPECIAL PLACE TO VISIT

El Cuartelejo

Many years ago (in the 1660's, it is believed) Indians fled from New Mexico to escape the harsh Spanish rule. They settled in western Kansas where they built a house or **pueblo.** The house probably looked like this:

In the early 1700's the Indians abandoned the house. It fell into ruins and was forgotten. Then, in 1889, archeaologists found the ruins of the pueblo.

Today you can visit the site of El Cuartelejo and see the ruins of this ancient house.

El Cuartelejo is 12 miles north of Scott city in Scott County.

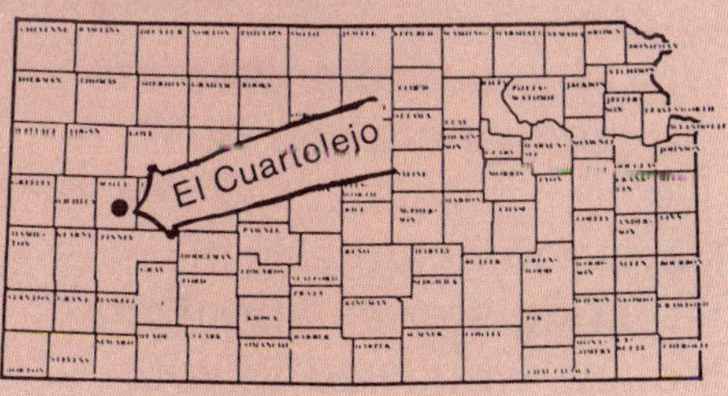

Chapter Eleven:
People of the South Wind

Who were the "people of the South Wind"? They were, of course, the Kansa Indians who lived in eastern Kansas. The State is named after these Indians.

It is very important to know about the Indians who lived in Kansas. They are very significant people in your Kansas Heritage.

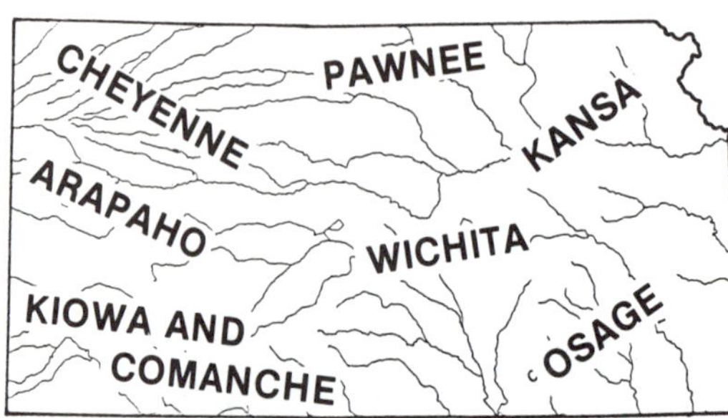

Indians who lived in Kansas about the year 1800.

There are several things you should know about the Indians. First, there were many tribes of Indians which lived in Kansas. Study the map above. Can you name the tribes of Indians who lived in Kansas in 1800?

* What Indian tribe lived on the land where you now live?
* Have you heard any interesting stories about the Indians who lived in your part of Kansas? Share these stories with the class.
* Are there places or things in your county or community which are named for the Indians? Make a list of the Indian names you find and put the list on your class bulletin board.

Something else to remember. The Indians who are shown on the map probably had not been in Kansas very long.

Look at the next map, please. This map shows you where the Indians came from.

What does the map tell you?

It tells you that the Kansa and Osage Indians once lived in Ohio, in the eastern part of the United States. The Cheyenne and Arapaho lived in Minnesota, then moved west through the Dakotas and Wyoming before they came to Kansas.

The Kiowa and Comanche once lived in the mountains of Montana, while the Pawnee and Wichita Indians originated in the country southwest of Kansas.

Can you think of the reasons why the Indians moved?

"One thing to remember about the Indians of Kansas is that most of them came to Kansas from other parts of our country."

The Kansa, Osage and Pawnee Indians who lived in the eastern part of Kansas were village Indians.

The houses in which they lived were called earthlodges. An earthlodge is made by covering a framework of branches with sod and dirt.

The outside walls of the lodge were about eight feet high. A domed roof covered the circular house. A hole in the middle of the roof allowed smoke from the cooking fire to escape.

You can easily see why the houses were called earthlodges—they looked as though they were piles of earth.

The village Indians built their lodges on high ground near a river or stream. Around the village lay the gardens where the Indian women raised crops. The men prepared the ground for planting—the women did all the rest of the work.

The Indian women did not have garden tools like ours. They used sharp sticks to dig up the ground and to make holes for the seed. They pulled weeds with their hands.

The Indian women raised corn, beans, squash and sunflowers. Corn was their most important crop. Every spring before the corn was planted the Indians in the village had a big ceremony.

There was dancing and singing, and the village leaders prayed for good weather and a good corn crop.

Beyond the fields lay the pastures where the Indian boys watched the horse herd. The horse was an Indian's most valuable piece of property. No question about that. A young brave was as proud of his horse as your big brother is of his sports car!

It is important for you to remember that the Indians did not have horses before the Spanish came. And it was not until about 1700 (just about three hundred years ago) that the Indians obtained horses.

You see, the Spanish had a law that Indians could not raise or own horses. So long as the Indians did not have horses, the Spanish soldiers knew they could easily control them.

Before long, however, the Indians began to get horses. They stole horses from Spanish ranches, and they rounded up stray horses that had run away from their Spanish owners.

Pretty soon the Indians were raising their own horses. They drove some of their extra horses up north, to offer them to the Indians who did not own horses. These Indians, of course, wanted the horses very badly. They were willing to trade anything they had in order to get the horses.

Horses changed the way the Indians lived. With horses they could travel farther in search of buffalo. The horse made the Indian men better hunters and better warriors. In fact, the Indian determined how rich he was by the number of horses he owned.

Some questions for you to think about:

1. How did Indians hunt buffalo before they had horses?
2. How did the horse make buffalo hunting easier for the Indians?
3. What kind of weapon is this Indian using to kill the buffalo?
4. Was this a dangerous way to hunt buffalo? What could happen to the Indian hunter?

Now you know why the Indian boys watched the horses very, very carefully. They didn't want any of the valuable animals to wander off or to be stolen.

A piece of flat ground near the village was used by the children as a playing field. The Indians loved to play games. Indian boys had a great time racing their ponies. All of the children, boys and girls, ran races on foot. They wanted to see who the fastest runners in the village were.

The Indians enjoyed having company, and visitors to the village received a warm and friendly welcome. Visitors were seated in a place of honor in one of the big earthlodges. One more person didn't make much difference—not when there were thirty or forty persons already living in the earthlodge.

The best food was prepared for the visitor. Usually the main dish was made from corn and meat. For **very** important guests, the Indians prepared a dish of delicious stew—made from a fat puppy!

Women of the village had many jobs. They worked in the fields. They prepared food and clothing. The women also made clay pots, wove baskets and made tools from bone and wood.

The men prepared the fields for planting. Other than that, the men didn't have other chores in the village. They spent their time talking and planning hunting trips. They also talked about forming war parties and raiding enemy camps to take horses. Much of their time was spent in training their horses and making weapons.

Indian parents loved their children, and they enjoyed playing with them.

The older children in the village had many things to

do. They learned to sing Indian songs and to perform Indian dances. They were taught to play musical instruments, such as flutes, drums, whistles and rattles.

Dolls made from clay and corn cobs kept the little Indian girls happy. The boys liked to play games such as "snow snake." This game was played in the winter when there was snow on the ground. It was played by throwing a piece of bone decorated with feathers (this was the "snow snake") back and forth across the packed, hard snow.

The boys played another game with poles and hoops. In this game teams of boys tried to toss wooden hoops over a pole.

While the boys and girls played their games, they chewed gum made from milkweed pods! They acted and did many things just like modern children, didn't they?

Indian children did not go to school as you do. They learned by listening to stories told them by the older men and women of the village.

The children heard stories of famous battles and successful hunting trips. They listened to stories about the great men and women of their village. They heard stories which helped them understand the land and the wild animals that lived on the land.

Since the Indians did not have a written language, the history of the tribe and the village was preserved in these stories. As they listened to the old men and old women of the village tell these stories, the Indian children came to understand what it meant to be a part of the village and a part of the tribe. And they learned what they must do to help the village and its people in the future.

In the spring of the year the Indian village was a very busy place. Once the crops had been planted, the people in the village prepared for a very important trip—a trip into western Kansas to hunt buffalo.

Each year the people of a village would follow the same trail into the buffalo country. Do you live near one of those old Indian trails? There are many of these trails in Kansas.

The Indians prepared carefully for the long trip to the hunting grounds. The women made skin tipis and prepared food. The men got their weapons and their horses in shape and ready for the hunt.

Finally it was time to leave. The skin tipis and bundles of food were tied to long poles which the horses pulled. These were known as **travois** (tra-voy). You might think of the travois as the Indians' pickup trucks.

The long line of Indians, horses and travois left the village. Scouts led the way west along the familiar hunting trail.

A few months later the Indians returned to their village in eastern Kansas. If the hunt had been successful, they brought back packs of dried buffalo meat. In the late summer and early fall they harvested their crops; then they went out on a fall hunt.

With supplies of corn, beans, dried pumpkin and sunflower seeds, as well as dried buffalo meat, on hand, the village Indians were ready for the long winter months ahead.

Indian travois with camp equipment, food and children!

AN INTERESTING HISTORIC SITE TO VISIT

Pawnee Indian Village Museum,Republic County

This fine museum, which is operated by the Kansas State Historical Society, stands on a high bluff near the Republican River. Two hundred years ago a Pawnee village of earthlodges covered this hill. There were thirty or forty lodges. About a thousand Pawnee men, women and children lived in the village.

A Pawnee earth lodge.

After the Indians abandoned this village, the earthlodges tumbled down and were covered by grass and sod. Not many years ago archaeologists removed the dirt from the earthlodge sites, and they found many interesting things.

This large museum building was built over the site of one earthlodge. Inside the museum you can see the floor of the earthlodge. You can see the pieces of tools, bits of food, ashes from fires and many other things which the Indians left behind.

The Pawnee Indian Village Museum is an excellent place to learn about the Pawnee Indians.

Pawnee Indian Village Museum
Republic County

Chapter Twelve: Indians of the Western Plains

The Indians who lived on the grass-covered plains of western Kansas did not live in earthlodge villages. And they did not plant crops.

These plains Indians were *nomads*—that is, they wandered from place to place. Since they depended upon the buffalo for their food, the Indians followed the buffalo herds. The Indians made camp wherever they found buffalo to hunt.

The Indians of the plains lived in skin tents called *tipis*. These tents could be quickly set up and quickly taken down—just the thing for people who were constantly on the move.

Of course, the horse was very important to the plains Indians. Mounted on horses, the Indians could travel many miles over the prairie. And it was much easier to hunt buffalo from horseback than on foot.

The Indians used just about every part of the dead buffalo. They wasted nothing.

They used the buffalo hides to cover their tipis. The Indians slept on buffalo robes. The women made water buckets, kettles and harness from the leather. Strips of hide were made into string, and the long buffalo hair was woven into strong ropes.

They carved spoons from the buffalo horns, and made glue from the hooves of the animals. Leg bones were used as rattles, and a dry hide, pulled tightly over a hollow log, made a drum used in dances and ceremonies.

Just about everything the Indians needed came from the buffalo. I guess you could say that the buffalo was the Indians' supermarket.

A camp of plains Indians. See the meat drying on the rack?

Indian boys began to ride horses when they were very small. In a few years they were excellent riders. Imagine the skill it took to hunt buffalo from horseback. And just keep in mind that the Indians usually rode bareback—without saddles!

And another thing: it took two hands to use the bow and arrow. So, as he galloped alongside the buffalo, the Indian hunter was not hanging on to his horse in any way—except with his legs.

The Indian horses, particularly those used to hunt buffalo, were well trained. They knew exactly what to do during the hunt. White men who saw the Indians hunt buffalo were amazed by the skill of both the hunters and the ponies.

While they were hunting buffalo the plains Indians traveled in small family bands. Several times a year, however, the family bands came together to make a large camp.

Then the Indians had feasts and celebrations. The

Indians loved to give parties, and there was something to do all the time the Indians were camped together. They sang and they danced around the campfires. They thanked the Great Spirit for sending the buffalo and for giving them a successful hunt.

The leaders of the tribe were chosen from the men who had shown ability and bravery in both the hunt and in war. An Indian tribe had many different leaders. Some leaders were in charge of the hunting parties. Others led the men on raids against their enemies.

These plains Indians were great warriors. From time to time war parties left the camp. As a rule their goal was to steal horses from their enemies. Men who entered the enemies' camps and made away with horses were considered the bravest men in the tribe. It took great daring and nerve to steal horses.

Women had important roles in the tribe, too. Wives and mothers were treated with respect. They were looked up to, and they made many decisions concerning the family. In some tribes all of the property in the tipi belonged to the women.

Some of you probably wonder how many Indians lived in Kansas in these early days.

There is no way of knowing for sure. But in the year 1844 white men in Kansas estimated that there were about 34,000 Indian men, women and children living in what is now Kansas.

Yes, the Indian population was very small. All of the Indians in Kansas in 1844 amounted to about one-quarter of the people who live in the city of Topeka today!

◀Cheyenne Tipis

Sac & Fox Bark House

Tonganoxie - a Delaware Leader

A Pawnee Brave▶

It is fun to learn about the Indians who lived in Kansas. They are very interesting people. I know you will want to learn more about the Indians who lived in your part of Kansas.

Go to your People Bank. Perhaps you have the names of men and women who can tell you stories about the Indians. If there are Indian men and women living in your community, invite them to your class and have them tell you about their people.

In many Kansas communities there are people who can teach you Indian dances and Indian crafts. I know you would welcome them to your class.

One important thing about the Indians—they understood the land.

The Indians lived through hot, dry summers and winter blizzards. The village Indians learned to raise crops. Both the village Indians and the plains Indians were excellent hunters.

They learned to travel across the vast prairies. They learned to talk by sign language with Indians of other tribes. And Indian hunters and warriors used mirrors and camp fires to send messages across the prairie.

"ATTENTION, ALL YOU HERITAGE HUNTERS! Did you know that you can discover your heritage while riding in your family car?"

"Yes, you can. All you have to do is play a game we call License Plate History."

All Kansas cars and trucks carry license plates. The letters on the license plates tell us what county the vehicle is registered in. Look at this license plate:

KANSAS
RP 1988

RP stands for Republic County. So we know that the owner of this car lives in Republic County.

As you ride in your family car watch for the license plates shown at the right. They will remind you of some important people in your Kansas heritage—for each of the counties is named for a tribe of Indians.

KANSAS CN 1234	Cheyenne County
KANSAS CM 5678	Comanche County
KANSAS KW 2580	Kiowa County
KANSAS OS 1206	Osage County
KANSAS PN 5201	Pawnee County
KANSAS WH 3901	Wichita County
KANSAS NO 2845	Neosho County

The name of this county comes from an Osage Indian word meaning "dirty or muddy water." The county is named for the Neosho River.

Chapter Thirteen:
Eastern Indians and the Missionaries

There is another part of the story of the Indians which needs to be told. This is the story of the Indians who were forced to come to live in Kansas.

It is not a very happy story. The Indians suffered greatly both during their hard journeys to Kansas and after they arrived in the new land.

But it is also the story of some fine white people—the missionaries who wanted very much to help the Indians have a better life.

The Spanish explorers and the French traders, as you know, found Indians living in what is now Kansas. If you have forgotten the names of these Indians look at the map on page 56.

There weren't very many of these Indians, and they were scattered over a vast country.

The years passed and in 1804 the United States purchased a huge piece of land from France. This is known as the Louisiana Purchase. Look at the map: you see that Kansas was part of the Louisiana Purchase.

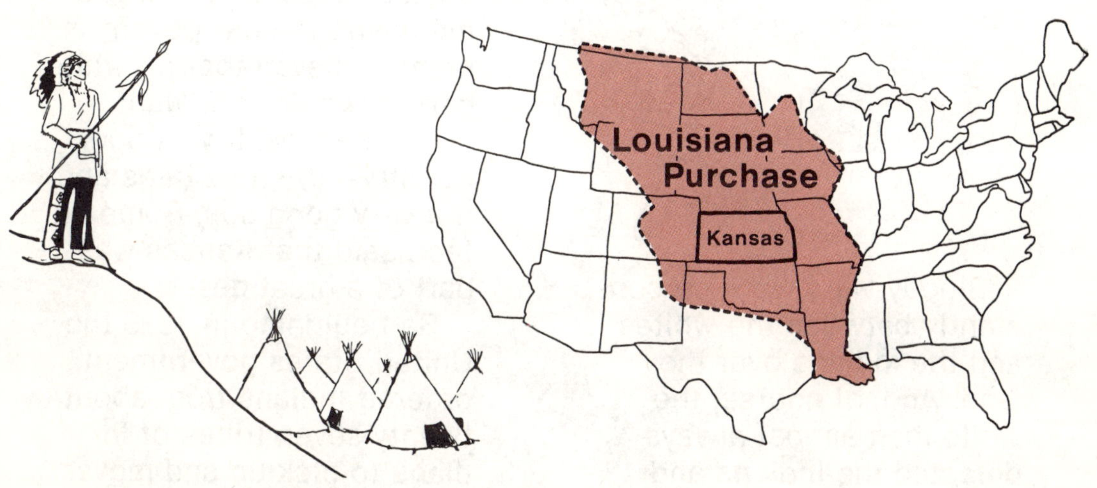

All this time the American people were moving west from the Atlantic coast, where the first colonies had been built. The land-hungry pioneers pushed the Indians before them.

Bloody wars went on constantly between the whites and the Indians over the land. And, of course, the white men almost always defeated the Indians and drove the Indians from the land they wanted.

Something had to be done to help the Indians—but what could be done?

Isaac McCoy, a Baptist minister, was one of many Americans who said that the Indians in the eastern part of the nation should be moved to another place. They had to be moved to a place where the white settlers would leave them alone. A place where the Indians could live in peace.

Where was this place?

Isaac McCoy thought that the best place for the Indians was the land west of the Missouri River—especially in Kansas.

After all, there was a huge amount of vacant land in Kansas. There would be ample room for the Eastern Indians. Moreover, the white men, who ran our government, believed that no white person would ever want to live in Kansas. It was poor country—dry, few trees and not very good soil. Some, in fact, said that Kansas was part of a great desert.

So beginning in 1825 the United States government ordered Indians from about twenty-seven tribes of Indians to pick up and move to Kansas.

In the meantime the government had signed treaties with the Osage and Kansa Indians. These Indians agreed to give up some of their lands, which would be divided among the Eastern Indians.

Look at this map. You can see that just about the entire eastern third of what is now the state of Kansas was divided up among the Indians.

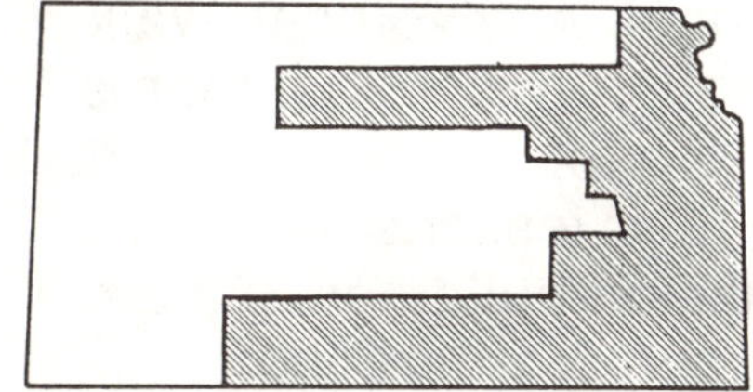

Indian Claims in Kansas 1846

The Eastern Indians started for Kansas. It was a long, difficult journey for many of them. The Ottawa Indians, for example, had to travel all the way from Wisconsin and Illinois. About one half of the tribe died on the way.

Living conditions weren't much better for the Indians once they got to Kansas. For many of the Indians, the Kansas climate was hard to take. Disease swept through the families, and, worse yet, greedy white traders hung around the Indian camps and sold whiskey to the men.

What few white persons realized at this time was that among the ten thousand or so Indians who were brought to Kansas there were many Indians who were well "civilized." Especially among the Delaware, Shawnee and Wyandot Indians there were persons who had lived among the whites for years. They could read and write; and many had married white persons. But they, too, were made to move to Kansas.

Now there were some white people who were concerned about the Indians. Many missionaries, men and women, came to work among the Indians. They tried to protect the Indians against white people who would have robbed them of their lands and money. The missionaries also set up schools where the Indian children could receive an education. And they opened churches where they taught the Indians about the Christian way of life.

These white missionaries must be counted among the heroes and heroines of Kansas history. To discover the story of these brave missionaries you must visit three historic sites maintained by the Kansas State

Historical Society: the Kaw Mission at Council Grove; the Shawnee Mission in Fairway; and the Iowa, Sac and Fox Mission near Highland.

There were many mission stations established among the Indians. Just about every church sent missionaries, but let's take a look at these three mission stations which you can visit today.

In Council Grove stands the Kaw, or Kansa, Mission. This mission and school was established in 1849 by Thomas S. Huffaker. While he and his helpers were not very successful in their attempts to educate the Indian children, Huffaker was able to keep peace between the Indians and the white settlers who moved onto the Indians' lands as the years passed.

The Shawnee Mission was established in 1830 by a Methodist minister, Thomas Johnson. Many of the buildings remain from the mission which was set up to educate Indian children. You can walk through the rooms where the Indian boys and girls lived while they attended school. And you can walk through the school rooms where the children attended to their lessons. Near the mission buildings is a small cemetery where the Reverend Johnson is buried.

In northeastern Kansas stands the Iowa, Sac and Fox Mission. It was founded in 1837 by a Presbyterian missionary, Samuel M. Irvin and his wife. Several other white couples usually worked with the Irvins, and each couple received a salary of $200 a year. It was discouraging work. The Indians refused to give up their old ways. Log cabins were built for the Indians to live in; the Indians used the logs for firewood. As happened at most mission schools, the Indian parents were reluctant to let their children attend the school.

Mr. Irvin, with the help of several helpers, printed school books in the Indian languages, but even that didn't help.

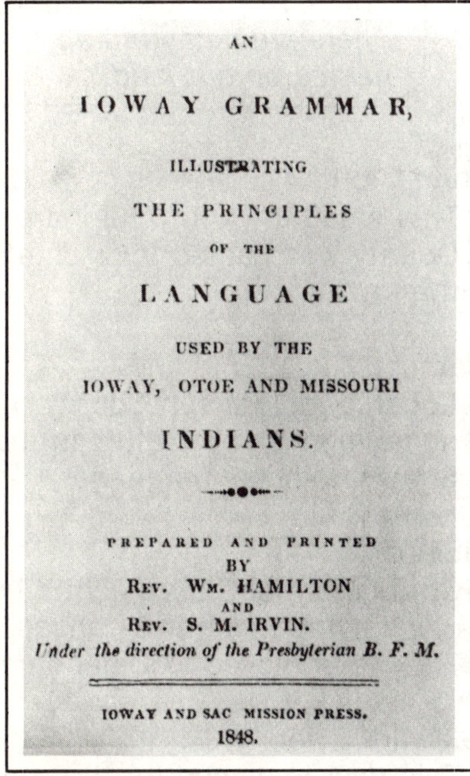

AN

IOWAY GRAMMAR,

ILLUSTRATING

THE PRINCIPLES

OF THE

LANGUAGE

USED BY THE

IOWAY, OTOE AND MISSOURI

INDIANS.

PREPARED AND PRINTED

BY

REV. WM. HAMILTON

AND

REV. S. M. IRVIN.

Under the direction of the Presbyterian B. F. M.

IOWAY AND SAC MISSION PRESS.

1848.

By the 1850's white settlers had taken over the land. The Indians were gone, and the mission closed down.

If you live in eastern Kansas, there is probably the site of a historic Indian mission not far from you. Go to your People Bank and find someone who can take you to see this important site and who can tell you about the Indians and missionaries.

One of my favorite historic places in Kansas is a little cemetery, not far from the city of Ottawa.

Close by this cemetery there once stood the buildings used by Baptist missionaries who had come to live among the Ottawa Indians.

In this cemetery you will find the graves of Christian Indians. You'll see the graves of Mr. and Mrs. Jotham Meeker, missionaries to the Indians. They came here in 1837. Mr. Meeker was a printer, and on his printing press he turned out a book in the Ottawa language. He also taught the boys how to farm. His wife nursed the sick women and children.

There is also the grave of John Tecumseh Jones, or Tauy Jones as he was known, an Indian minister who loved his people.

What happened to these Indians?

In time almost all of the Indians were ordered to leave Kansas—once again to move to a new place.

As the Indians left Kansas, their lands were taken up by white settlers.

Today there are only three small Indian reservations left in Kansas. These reservations are shown on the following map.

Present Indian Reservations in Kansas.

White Cloud:
This small town in Doniphan County was named for a chief of the Iowa tribe.

Olathe:
Located in Johnson County, this name means "beautiful" in the Shawnee Indian language.

Wichita:
Coronado found the Wichita Indians living in central Kansas. They later moved to Oklahoma.

Delaware River:
This river is named for the Delaware Indians, one of the Eastern tribes which was moved to Kansas.

Tonganoxie:
This town in Leavenworth County is named for a Delaware chief.

Chetopa:
Located in Labette County, this city is named for an Osage chief.

UNIT FIVE:
PIONEER TRAILS

Chapter Fourteen
Exploring the Plains

You already know about the Spanish and French explorers and traders who traveled over Kansas centuries ago. These brave men learned a great deal about the prairie and about the Indians who lived on the land.

But in the United States (which was then made up of a few States along the Atlantic coast) people knew very little about the western prairies.

So after President Jefferson arranged the Louisiana Purchase, he decided to send some men to have a look at the land which our nation had bought.

To lead this expedition President Jefferson selected Meriwether Lewis and William Clark. The President told them to form an expedition, go up the Missouri River, cross the Rocky Mountains and reach the Pacific Ocean. What a challenge! But Lewis and Clark were not afraid. They rounded up about forty men—including a Black man by the name of York—and in the spring of 1804 left St. Louis to follow the Missouri River across the plains to the Rocky Mountains.

Here is how the men of the Lewis and Clark party moved their heavy keelboat, loaded with their supplies and equipment, up the Missouri River. Notice that the men are walking along the shore. They are pulling the heavy boat upstream. This is known as **cordelling**, and you can imagine how hard work it was. And they worked from dawn to dark.

July 4

June 26

Lewis & Clark in Kansas

On June 26, 1804, the expedition camped near the spot where the Kansas River empties into the Missouri River. Hunters were sent out, and they returned with seven deer for the men to cook and eat. These deer were killed on the spot where Kansas City stands today!

The men slowly made their way up the river. On July 4th they camped near a creek which they named Independence Creek, in honor of that day. They even took time for a little celebrating. The city of Atchison grew up near this spot.

The Lewis and Clark expedition is one of the most important events in American history. These great explorers crossed the continent. They had the important help of an Indian woman, Sacagawea, who guided them through the mountains. They saw country no white man had ever seen. Like all pioneers, they "prepared the way for others."

Since they stayed close to the Missouri River, Lewis and Clark really didn't see much of Kansas.

Lewis and Clark

But in 1806 Zebulon Pike, an officer in the United States Army, set out with a small group of soldiers to explore the prairie land that lay west of the Missouri River.

Pike bought horses from the Osage Indians in eastern Kansas, and headed out into the prairie.

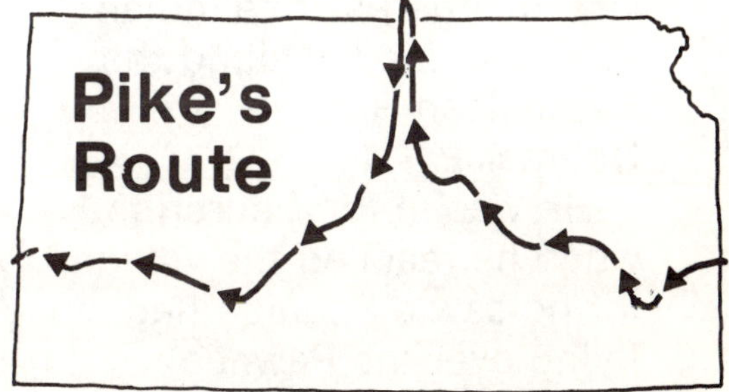

For sixty-six days Pike and his men traveled in what is now Kansas. And they saw some amazing sights! One day in eastern Kansas, for example, they looked over the prairie and saw herds of buffalo, elk, deer and antelope. As they marched along the Cottonwood River they were never out of sight of a huge herd of buffalo. And near Garden City they were amazed to see immense herds of buffalo and wild horses grazing quietly on the prairie.

It was easy to kill wild animals for food. During their trip across Kansas Pike's men killed forty-nine buffalo, seventeen deer, nine antelope, six elk, three turkeys and some prairie dogs. Pike said that the cooked prairie dog meat tasted like squirrel.

Look at the map carefully. You'll notice that after crossing the eastern part of Kansas Pike and his men turned north. Pike wanted to visit a large Pawnee Indian village which lay along the Republican River in Nebraska.

He was in for a surprise when he reached the village, for he saw a Spanish flag flying over the Pawnee earthlodges. He found out that a large Spanish army had just left the village. The Indians were impressed with the well-equipped Spanish soldiers. And here came Pike with just a handful of ragged, dirty Americans.

Do you know what Pike did? He began to tell the Indians about the United States. He said that since the Indians lived on land which now belonged to the United States, they should take down the Spanish flag and raise the American flag in its place.

The Indians must have been impressed with Pike's brave talk, for they lowered the Spanish flag and put up the flag Pike gave them. The American flag fluttered in the breeze over the Indian village.

A monument to Zebulon Pike and his men stands at the Pawnee Indian Village Museum in Republic County. The Pawnee village where the flag incident took place is located northwest of this museum near Red Cloud, Nebraska.

Look at the map again. After Pike left the Pawnee village you'll notice that he headed south until he came to the Arkansas River. Then he followed that river west into Spanish territory. Spanish soldiers captured Pike and his men and put them in prison for a time. After they were released they returned to the United States to report on their adventures in the West.

What did Pike tell the people about the land of Kansas?

To tell you the truth, he didn't think much of Kansas. He was impressed with all the wild animals he saw, and he said that Kansas some day might be a good place to raise cattle and sheep. But he didn't think farmers would ever be able to live on the land. The soil did not appear to be fertile. In fact, much of Kansas, according to Pike, appeared to be a sandy desert. And since there were few trees in the country, settlers would always have a real problem finding fuel.

All in all Pike did not think Kansas would ever be settled by large numbers of Americans.

Zebulon Pike, who visited the "deserts" of Kansas.

Other American explorers, who came to Kansas after Pike, pretty much agreed with his conclusions. Kansas was part of the "great desert" which lay between the Missouri River and the Rocky Mountains. It was a land with very little rain; a treeless prairie; and land without a future.

About this time a famous United States Senator, Daniel Webster, gave a speech in Washington. Here is what he had to say about Kansas and the West:

"What do we want with this vast and worthless area, of this region of savages and wild beasts, of deserts, of shifting sands and whirlwinds, of dust, of cactus and prairie dogs; to what use could we ever hope to put these great deserts?"

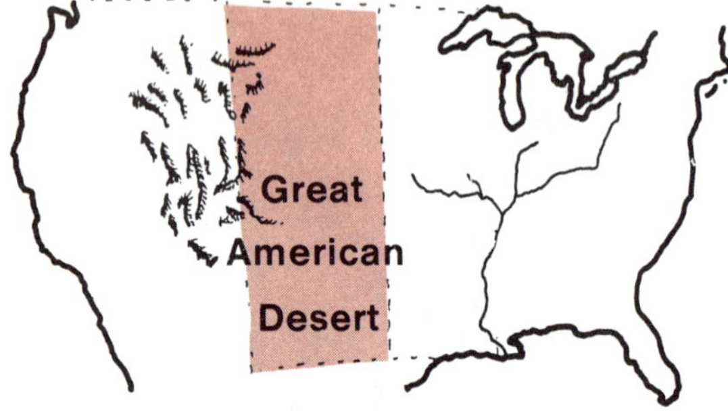

Don't you wonder how these men reached the conclusion that Kansas was a desert country? Let me help you understand what the men of this generation were thinking about.

First of all, you must remember that Kansas, in 1806, did not look anything at all as it does today. The farmers and ranchers who have come to Kansas have really improved the land. For one thing they planted the trees which grow all over Kansas today.

And you must remember that Pike and the other American explorers were from the East. Back in that country there are huge forests and lots of rain. It isn't hard to imagine how shocked they were when they saw the treeless Kansas prairie. It must have looked strange and terrible to them.

Since there were few trees, the explorers wondered what settlers would use for fuel. You see, even in the early 1800's people thought about their energy needs.

Another reason the prairies were unattractive was because of the prairie fires which roared over the land. The earth often was covered with black ashes. When the wind blew—which is quite often in Kansas —the dirt would rise in huge clouds. And the explorers thought they were in the middle of a dry desert!

And remember: a huge herd of buffalo would eat every blade of grass in sight. The buffalo undoubtedly helped make the land appear desolate.

It is no wonder these explorers concluded that the land of Kansas was worthless. The country had no value—except as a good place for Indians. Yes, since white people would probably never want the land, it was obviously a good place to stick the Indians. The Indians would never be bothered by white people again—by land-hungry whites who wanted the Indians out of the way.

So, as you have learned, the government decided to bring thousands of Indians to Kansas—to live in the "great desert."

The land had one other use, however. Beyond Kansas there was a city known as Santa Fe. It was an important Spanish city, and its residents were said to be very rich. Americans wanted to visit the city and find out if the people wanted to purchase American goods. And these traders laid out a trail that ran across Kansas. It crossed the prairie and desert and was known as the Santa Fe trail.

"Yes, there was one good thing about the land of Kansas. It made a good highway for folks who wanted to go west!"

SOME FUN THINGS TO DO!

1. Read about the Lewis and Clark expedition and the journey of Zebulon Pike. Make a report to the class about the adventures these men had in the West.
2. Tell the story of Sacagawea, the Indian woman who guided Lewis and Clark through the mountains. And see if you can find out anything about York, the Black man who accompanied Lewis and Clark.
3. Pretend you are a TV news reporter. Ask your classmates to pretend that they are Mr. Lewis, Mr. Clark, or Mr. Pike, who have just returned from their explorations. Interview the explorers, just as a modern TV reporter would do.

Chapter Fifteen
The Road to Santa Fe

There are many historical markers in Kansas. Have you ever taken the time to read the historical markers that are near your school? Don't be like the one little girl I met in a Kansas school. She said to me, "Dr. Manley, I know what a historical marker is."

"You do?" I replied, "What is a historical marker?"

"Well," she said, "A historical marker is that thing Daddy drives by and says some day we'll stop to read."

I hope you don't feel that way about historical markers, for these markers are very important and interesting.

For example, this is one of the stone markers that tell us the story of the Santa Fe trail . . . one of the most important pioneer trails in American history.

The Santa Fe trail started at a number of points in Missouri. Steamboats brought trade goods, such as metal tools and clothing, up the Missouri River. At Westport, Independence and other river towns, the goods were taken from the steamboats and loaded into huge wagons. Drawn by oxen or mules, the wagons then started over the long trail to Santa Fe, New Mexico.

Why did the American traders want to go to Santa Fe? Mainly because there was a good profit to be made in the trade.

You see, the Mexican people who lived in Santa Fe at this time, were under the rule of Spain. The Spanish rulers said that the people had to buy all their goods from Spain. Look at this map and you'll see the problem the residents of Santa Fe had to deal with:

The goods they wanted had to come all the way across the Atlantic Ocean from Spain. After entering Mexico at Vera Cruz, the goods had to travel hundreds of miles north to Santa Fe.

On the other hand, notice that Westport, in Missouri, U.S.A., was a good deal closer. So, the people of Santa Fe were anxious to trade with the merchants of Missouri.

The Spanish government did everything possible to keep Americans out of Santa Fe. Traders who tried to sneak into New Mexico were arrested and put in prison.

In 1821, however, the situation changed. In that year a Missouri trader, William Becknell by name, went west to round up wild horses and to trade with the Indians. Somewhere out on the prairie Becknell and his Americans met some Mexican soldiers. The soldiers told them that Mexico had revolted against Spain. Mexico was now a free nation, and this meant that the road to Santa Fe was open to American traders.

Even though they had very few trade goods, the Americans hurried to Santa Fe. There they received a warm welcome. The Americans sold their goods quickly and returned home with gold Mexican coins jingling in their saddlebags.

You can imagine how excited the American traders were! And next year William Becknell went to Santa Fe for a second time. For this trip he used wagons to carry some of his trade goods.

Becknell crossed eastern Kansas to the Arkansas River. He then followed the river into southwestern Kansas, where he decided to cross the Arkansas and take a shortcut to Santa Fe.

Look at the map again. The safer trail was the one that followed the Arkansas River into Colorado. But Becknell wanted a shorter route, so he crossed the Arkansas and headed into the desolate, dry country which lay south of the river. Becknell and his men almost died along this trail, which Spanish and Mexican traders called "The Journey of Death." The Americans ran out of water. They were dying of thirst. They cut open the veins in their mules' ears and drank the blood. One day hunters killed a buffalo. Crazed by thirst, the men leaped on the dead animal—not to eat its meat, but to rip open the stomach and drink the filthy water that was inside the stomach!

This stretch of trail, known as the Cimarron Cutoff, was terribly hard. Oldtimers insisted that jackrabbits in this country carried three days' food supply and two canteens of water. That's a joke—but there was no joking about the hardships endured by the first travelers on this cut-off.

The Santa Fe trade grew rapidly! In just a few years hundreds of traders were active in the trade. They used huge wagons which carried two or three tons of cargo. At first the traders used mules to pull their wagons, but finally most of them decided that oxen worked better. Although oxen were slower than mules, they were tougher than mules and much easier to handle.

A Santa Fe caravan on the trail.

This is a photograph of Alexander Majors, one of the best known Santa Fe traders.

Alexander grew up on a farm in Missouri, but he decided to try his hand at running a freight line to Santa Fe.

In 1848 he took his first wagons over the trail. He had six wagons, each loaded with about two tons of goods. He made the trip from Missouri to Santa Fe, and back to Missouri, in ninety-two days—a record that stood for many years. He made a good profit from this first trip, and next year he returned to Santa Fe with twenty wagons.

Mr. Majors was a Christian gentleman, and he gave to each of his employees a Bible. He insisted that his men obey the rules he had written. Here are some of the instructions he gave the the leaders of his wagon trains:

1. Do not allow the men to whip their teams at all.
2. The use of profane language is strictly forbidden.
3. We expect our trains to observe the Sabbath, and whenever an opportunity occurs to hear preaching, embrace it.
4. We want our men to pay due respect to all persons they meet on the road, whether Indians or whites, as many difficulties occur from abuse and insult offered to inoffensive people.

Read rule No. 4 carefully. If all the traders had followed Major's rule, there would have been much less bloodshed along the trail. We'll discuss the Indians and the traders in just a minute.

The Santa Fe caravan on the Kansas trail.

In the 1830's and 1840's the Santa Fe trade became big business. Let's talk now about how the wagon trains operated on this important trail.

The traders loaded their wagons in Independence, Westport (which is not part of Kansas City, Missouri), or some other Missouri River town.

As soon as the prairie grass was high enough in the spring to provide food for the mules and oxen, the traders set off.

Since there was little danger from hostile Indians in eastern Kansas, the traders traveled alone or in small groups.

During the first days on the trail the men had to be very careful with their animals. The mules and oxen always tried to run away and return to their warm stables and good pastures. There is one canyon in eastern Kansas where more than a thousand oxen died in a stampede. So the traders had to be careful; they certainly didn't want to have their animals run off and kill themselves!

The men walked beside the wagons during the day. Those who drove mules were called "mule-skinners." The men who handled oxen were called "bullwhackers," because they carried long wooden sticks with which they "whacked" the oxen. Most of the bullwackers also had long whips. They could perform amazing tricks with their whips. It is said that experts could kill a fly on the back of an oxen—and never touch the hide of the animal.

The traders kept an eye on the sky. They wanted enough rain to help the grass to grow; but they didn't want storms. Heavy rains flooded the prairies and made it impossible to take the heavy wagons across the streams. It might take a wagon train a whole day to cross a stream, which we whizz across in an automobile today in just a second or two.

The traders always crossed a creek or river before making camp. If a storm came up during the night the stream would flood and it might be impossible for the wagons to cross for days.

Eastern Kansas was also the home of the most bloodthirsty insects in the world—at least that's what the traders said. The gnats, mosquitoes and other insects were a terrible problem. The men often covered their animals with blankets to keep the insects off. Many stampedes were caused by animals who had been driven crazy by insect stings.

During the night the men made fires from wet wood. They tried to sleep in dense

clouds of smoke, which were supposed to keep the bugs away.

As the traders passed over the trail, they named the landmarks they saw. For example, one creek was named 110 Mile Creek. At this point the traders calculated that they were about 110 miles from their starting point in Independence, Missouri.

If the weather cooperated. and the prairie trail remained dry, the wagons could cover fifteen to twenty miles a day. So after a little more than a week after leaving Independence or Westport, the wagons would approach a very important place along the trail—Council Grove.

Representatives of the United States had met with the Indians who lived in eastern Kansas at this spot in 1825. The Indians agreed to let the wagons pass over the land.

Council Grove was a wonderful camping spot. There were all the things the travelers needed—good water, a grove of trees, fine grass and stores and blacksmith shops.

The traders camped several days at Council Grove. They spent every minute preparing for the long trip ahead, across the Kansas prairie and the distant mountains, to Santa Fe.

One man who kept a store in Council Grove kept track of the men and animals who passed through the town in 1858. Here is his list: 2,440 men; 1,827 wagons; 15,174

Council Grove and Wagons

oxen; and 9,608 tons of supplies, valued at at least 3.5 million dollars.

While camped at Council Grove the traders held a very important meeting.

Robert Manley and Council Oak

Under the spreading branches of a huge oak tree —only the stump of which can be seen today— the traders came together and organized for the trip across the plains. Because of the Indian danger, they knew that it was best to have all the wagons form one large train or caravan.

During the meeting the men elected their leaders and they adopted a set of rules. One rule they all agreed upon—every man in the wagon train had to take his turn at night guard duty!

Finally the men were ready to start out. Before the sun came up the leader of the caravan yelled, "Turn out! Turn out!" That was the signal for all the men to jump from their blankets that had been spread on the ground.

Then came the loud cry, "Catch up!" which was the signal for the men to round up their animals and hitch them to their wagons.

Just as the sun rose above the horizon there would be another call—"Stretch out!" Whips popped, men yelled, oxen bellowed —and the wagons began to roll—on their way to Santa Fe.

The wagons would roll until about ten o'clock in the morning. Then the men made camp. The animals were turned loose on the prairie to graze.

Through the hottest part of the day the men and animals rested. Then, about three or four o'clock in the afternoon, the animals were hitched to the wagons again and the caravan traveled until nearly dark.

The best campsites were those that lay near a good spring of water. A favorite spot of the traders was known as Diamond Springs, because the sparkling water that gushed from the springs looked like diamonds.

Along the trail enterprising men built what were known as "road ranches." William D. Wheeler, for example, had such an establishment at the point where the Santa Fe trail crossed the Little Arkansas River. In 1861 he placed the following advertisement in the Council Grove newspaper:

NOTICE: LITTLE ARKANSAS RANCHE
The traveling public are respectfully informed that the undersigned is located on the Little Arkansas, where the great Santa Fe road crosses the same. I keep always on hand, Provisions, Groceries and Liquors, also are prepared to accomodate travelers. I have several large stone corrals for penning stock. Also have built a strong and substantial bridge across the Little Arkansas, for the accomodation of the traveling public.

William D. Wheeler

Farther west on the trail was another ranche operated by W.M. Mathewson, who was called "Buffalo Bill" Mathewson.

Robert Manley at crossing and ranche site.

"Buffalo Bill" built his ranche where the trail crossed Cow Creek. Indians attacked the ranche in 1864, but Bill and his employees drove them off. Bill and the boys then rode to help a nearby wagon train which was under attack. When Bill was gone, the ranch was run by his wife, Elizabeth, who was a crack shot with both pistol and rifle.

A day or so after crossing Cow Creek, the caravan came in sight of the Arkansas River. Everyone in the wagon train was excited, for they were now in buffalo country. And when the first herd of buffalo was sighted, every man went crazy. They all caught a severe case of "buffalo fever." They jumped on their ponies and galloped off to shoot the buffalo.

Bringing down a mighty buffalo was not easy. Most of the hunters came back empty handed. One inexperienced hunter chased a buffalo over the prairie. As he closed in on the huge beast, he raised his rifle—fired—and shot his own horse in the back of the head! I imagine he took some kidding from his friends after that incident.

Around the campfires there would be many stories to be told about the buffalo. The old-timers would tell about their hunting experiences; there would be tales about the mysterious white buffalo; about the critter that had four horns; and the scary tale of the "ghost buffalo" which roamed close to the wagon trains and talked to the men on guard duty—in a woman's voice! Yes, sir, lots of stories to tell.

"Catch up!" "Stretch out!"

The wagons roll on again . . . day after long day.

"Look over there! That's Pawnee Rock."

All the men leave the wagon train and with their sharp knives carve their names in the rock.

The monument on top of Pawnee Rock.

"Be careful where ye walk!" The old-timers give the advice. This is rattlesnake country! And the reptiles are everywhere! Men with their whips walk in front of the caravan. They use their whips to kill the snakes that are in the road.

And at night, before the oxen and mules are allowed to graze, the pasture ground has to be cleared of rattlers, too.

Out here in western Kansas, however, the real problem is Indians!

The Santa Fe caravan often traveled in four columns, as you see in this old drawing.

In the event of an Indian attack the four columns of wagons could be quickly drawn into a circle. With the animals corraled inside the circle, the traders were prepared to stand off the Indian raiders.

Caravan in columns

In 1829 the Army sent soldiers to travel with the caravan. But these soldiers were infantry—soldiers who walk—and they couldn't do much against the horse-mounted Indians. A few years later, however, the Army had cavalry, horse-mounted soldiers, on duty along the trail.

The Army also built forts along the trail. Soldiers from the post were sent to patrol the trail and to help the travelers in any way they could. On this map you'll see the Army forts that were built during the days of the Santa Fe trail.

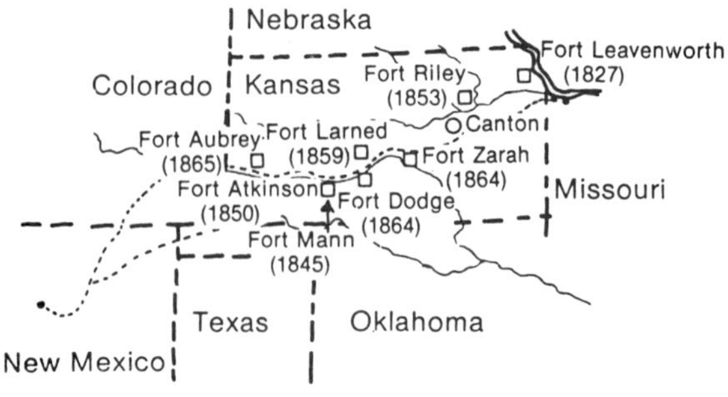

BLUECOATS ALONG THE SANTA FE TRAIL

Soldiers from Fort Riley helped protect the Santa Fe traders. Notice the statue of the cavalrymen -- a tribute to the bluecoats who served in pioneer Kansas.

Fort Dodge looked like this in 1867.

BLUECOATS

As I looked across the parade ground of old Fort Larned, I thought of all the soldiers who served here. The soldiers called Fort Larned, "Camp Alert," because they always seemed to be on alert for an Indian attack.

Ft. Larned has now been restored by the National Park Service. Be sure you visit this exciting historical sight!

The ground along the Santa Fe trail was soaked with the blood of both Indian warriors and white traders and soldiers.

In 1846 Indians attacked every wagon train on the trail. In 1847 Indian raiders killed 47 traders, destroyed 330 wagons and drove off 6,500 animals.

There were never enough soldiers to drive off the Indians; and the Indians were never strong enough to keep the white traders from crossing their land. So the fighting went on for years and years.

East of Canton, a pioneer cemetery is located where the Santa Fe trail once passed.

And in the cemetery is the grave of Ed Miller, aged 18 years, killed by Cheyenne Indians, July, 1865.

The long caravan rolled across the prairie. To the south lay the Arkansas River. Now the leaders of the caravan had a decision to make: should they follow the trail along the Arkansas River into Colorado, or should they cross the Arkansas and take the Cimarron cut-off?

Most of the wagon trains took the second choice. They crossed the Arkansas and followed the Cimarron cut-off. And in a few more weeks they were in Santa Fe! They had reached the end of one of America's great pioneer trails.

All told the traders covered about 750 miles of prairie and mountain trail—more than half of that distance was within the borders of what later became the State of Kansas.

The trail was very important. The Santa Fe trade encouraged Americans to think about the West. But more important, those who followed this trail learned how to travel by wagon across the vast prairie.

That knowledge came in handy during the 1840's when thousands of Americans, men, women, and children, heard about Oregon and California and decided to drive their wagons along the pioneer trails that led west.

Burlingame

Chapter Sixteen
Covered Wagon Pioneers

The year is 1848. It is late winter in Pike County, Missouri. A cold, damp wind howls around the little log cabin. Inside the cabin, sitting close to the crackling fire, Mrs. Bidwell and her two children, Jeremy and Jennie, listen carefully to Mr. Bidwell as he talks.

"Yes, I've made up my mind," Mr. Bidwell says firmly. "We are going to move to Oregon!"

"Where is Oregon, Daddy?" asks Jennie.

"What's in Oregon?" yells Jeremy. "Why are we going to Oregon?"

"Hold it," Mr. Bidwell says loudly. "Give me a minute and I'll tell you about Oregon. First of all, Oregon is a new country. It is a long way from Missouri, a very long way, clear across the prairie and the Rocky Mountains. But it is a fine country, with a wonderful climate. I'm told that crops grow very well. And most important, there is very little disease in Oregon."

Mr. Bidwell stopped for a moment and gazed into the fire. Then he said quietly, "We're going to Oregon because I think you children will have a future in that new country. And we'll get there by covered wagon—over the Oregon Trail."

The Bidwells don't have time to waste. They must be ready to leave for Oregon in the spring.

Mr. Bidwell went to town and talked to the wagon

maker. Since the wagon would be the family's home for the next five or six months, he wanted a well-built wagon. The wagon had to be strong to stand the hard wear of trail travel; and it had to be light, so the animals would not be worn out by pulling it.

Speaking of animals, Mr. Bidwell had a difficult time making up his mind about what kind of animals he would use to pull the wagon. Some men told him that horses or mules were best because they were faster than oxen. But the problem was that horses and mules were expensive. Besides, Indians would steal horses and mules every change they got; they usually left the oxen alone.

Like most folks who traveled the trail to Oregon, Mr. Bidwell bought six oxen for the wagon—four to pull the covered wagon and two to have as "spares," just in case.

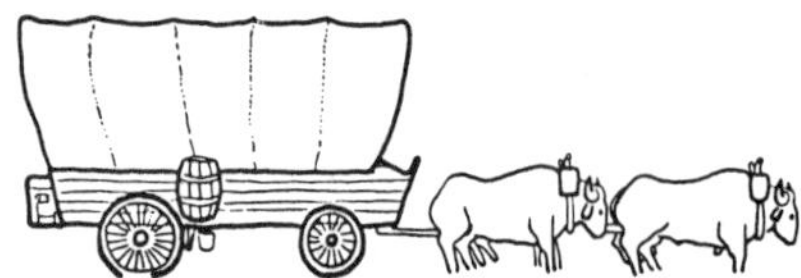

Mrs Bidwell is busy making preparations, too. First she selected the food they would carry with them. For her family—two adults and two children—Mrs. Bidwell figured she would need the following supplies:

800 pounds of flour
725 pounds of bacon
75 pounds of coffee
160 pounds of sugar
200 pounds of beans
150 pounds of dried fruit
25 pounds of salt
50 pounds of rice
50 pounds of cornmeal
1 keg of vinegar

Mrs. Bidwell had to figure out how to prepare and store all that food. She also decided that they would take the family milk cow along. They would have fresh milk and butter every day.

Mrs. Bidwell carefully selected the pots and pans she would need for cooking. She also bought a small iron stove in which to bake bread. All these utensils she put in a large wooden box. Each time they stopped for meals, Father Bidwell would take the box out of the wagon, and Mother would have everything she needed to prepare the meal.

Mother Bidwell also made up a medicine chest. Although she prayed that none of her family would be injured or become ill, she knew she had to be prepared. There were no doctors along the trail.

Then she packed strong, well-made clothing for everyone to wear. She also bought four pairs of goggles. She heard that trail dust was a terrible problem; and the ugly goggles would protect her family's eyes from the burning dust.

It is now the first of April. The new spring grass is up—the weather is warm.

Father Bidwell cracks his long whip over the backs of the strong oxen. The animals lean forward and begin to walk. The wagon lurches and begins to roll. Mother and Jennie sit firmly in the swaying seat. They are on their way to Oregon!

For the next week the Bidwell wagon follows the road across Missouri. The road is filled with wagons carrying other families west.

Finally, the Bidwells arrive in Independence, Missouri, where the Oregon trail begins. The town is filled with people who are waiting to begin the trip to Oregon.

Here is the town of Independence as it looked when the Bidwells arrived in their wagon.

While camped on the outskirts of town Mr. Bidwell meets other men who are going to Oregon. They agree to form a wagon train. There are fifteen families in the train—just about the right number.

The men elect Mr. Bidwell to be captain of the wagon train; and Mr. Bidwell calls a meeting in which the men write the rules for the wagon train. One rule says that every man must take his turn standing night guard over the animals. They don't want to take any chances with their animals. Without animals, the pioneers would be in serious trouble.

It is now the middle of April. The new grass is beginning to sprout. Mr. Bidwell rides out and looks at the prairie. He gallops back to camp.

"The grass looks fine to me," he calls out. "Tomorrow we will leave for Oregon."

No one sleeps very well that night. They are too excited. Before daylight everyone is up. The wagons are packed. The oxen are yoked. Just as the sun peeks over the horizon Mr. Bidwell gives the signal. The wagons slowly move into line. The waiting is over. In four or five months they will be in Oregon.

They leave the town of Independence behind them. The trail followed a long ridge. They came to a trail which came in from the north. This trail started in Westport, where hundreds of wagons were unloaded from steamboats to begin the trip to Oregon.

Westport Landing. Wagons preparing for the trip to Oregon.

The wagons slowly move on along the crowded trail. Clouds of dust fill the air. There are the sounds of oxen, creaking wagon wheels, children yelling. Everything is in a wonderful state of confusion and noise!

The wagons roll between several buildings. This is the Shawnee Mission. The Indian children, who are attending school at the Mission, stand beside the trail and watch the passing wagons. They wave to the white children who are peeking out from under the canvas wagon tops.

For several days the Bidwell's wagon followed a well-worn trail. It had been used for years by the wagons heading for Santa Fe.

Then they came to a fork in the trail. (The town of Gardner stands at this spot today.) They saw a signpost by the road. One sign pointed straight ahead and said: "To Santa Fe." Another sign pointed north and announced: "To Oregon." Mr. Bidwell, riding in front of the wagon train, turned the wagons on to this north road.

This marker stands near the spot where the Oregon Trail left the Santa Fe Trail.

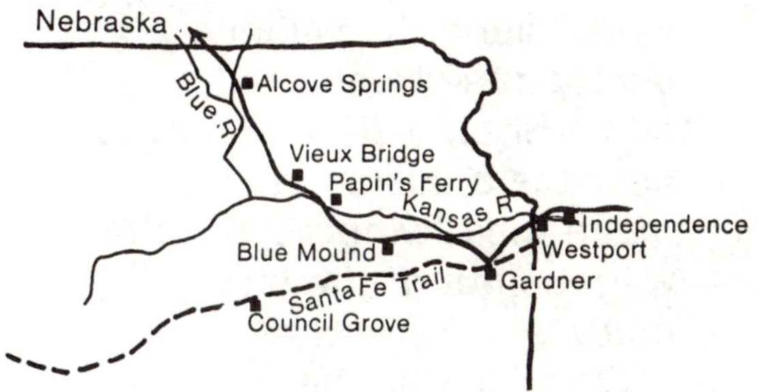

The wagons now roll across the Kansas prairie. The grass was a bright green. Bunches of wildflowers dotted the prairie. One man said, "Were the country only timbered, it would be the garden spot of the world."

The wagons rolled by Blue Mound. Today the Mound is covered with timber, but in the 1840's it was covered with grass. All the children from the wagon train ran to the top of the hill to get a look at the country. Their folks were angry. They didn't think they should be wasting time like this.

Blue Mound today.

The wagons and oxen splashed across the Wakarusa River. It was hard work taking the wagons across the stream. But some Shawnee Indians lived near the crossing, and they made their living pulling the wagons out of the sticky mud.

Once across the Wakarusa, the wagons swung north. They passed over a line of hills—today the campus of Kansas University and the city of Lawrence—and turned west to follow the Kansas River.

There was another twist in the trail and the wagon train stopped at the Kansas River. (They were right in the middle of Topeka.)

There was a ferry which operated across the Kansas River at this spot. It was run by Joseph and Louis Papin. The men carefully lowered the wagons down the bank with ropes. The wagons were pushed on to a ferry boat—a platform of planks on three wooden canoes. Then the crude ferry was poled across the river.

This is where the Papin ferry operated across the Kansas River.

The Papins usually charged $4.00 for each wagon, 25¢ for each mule and 10¢ for each person who rode their ferry. Most of the travelers let their animals swim across the muddy river. Only the people and the wagons took the boat.

The journey from Independence to the crossing of the Kansas River usually took eight days. And the pioneers had learned many lessons in these first days on the trail.

For example, some of the men found that they had loaded their wagons too heavily. The wagons were breaking down, and the animals could not pull the wagons through muddy spots and across streams.

So, they began to throw things out of their wagons —farm tools, furniture, extra clothing, spare food—anything they could throw away to lighten the load. The trail began to look like a gigantic junkpile!

The pioneers also learned not to waste time. There were always delays that they hadn't counted on. They might have to wait three or four days for a flooded stream to go down. So, on good days, they needed to cover ground. Their goal was no less than fifteen miles a day, every day.

Most of the wagon trains, however, did not travel on Sunday. That was the day of rest for both the people and their animals.

They also learned about the Kansas weather! Yes, indeed. One minute a bright, beautiful day. The next minute a terrible storm sweeping across the prairie. A downpour turned the trail into a sea of mud. The wind tore wagon covers to shreds. Lightning shattered the darkness and sent frightened mules and oxen stampeding off. After the storm passed men and boys spent hours trying to round up animals.

Mothers hated the storms because there was no way they could dry their families' clothing and bedding. And it was almost impossible to build a fire during the storms. One mother, camped near Papin's ferry, had her husband hold an umbrella over her and a small fire—while she baked a batch of hot biscuits.

Then there were the bugs! Millions of crickets, buffalo gnats and mosquitoes attacked the people and the animals. Some nights no one could sleep because of the buzzing, biting bugs. The men would build fires and the people tried to sleep in the clouds of smoke, hoping the smoke would keep the bugs away. One man wrote in his diary that the Kansas mosquitoes were "not as big as turkeys; none was larger than crows."

Something else the pioneers learned. It was not always easy to find a good camp site at the end of the day. There were hundreds of wagons on the trail, and this meant that hundreds of families were looking for places to camp at the end of the day.

Good water was hard to find. Wells along the trail were filled with filthy water. Bad water caused most of the sickness which befell the people on the trail.

And there were accidents, too. Children fell from the wagon and were run over by the heavy wheels. Men were injured by the animals. At every river crossing there was the danger of drowning in the swirling water. Guns were the cause of many accidents. Every family had several guns. They wanted to be ready for an Indian attack. But the pioneers soon realized that the loaded guns were more dangerous than the Indians. Hardly a day passed without someone getting shot accidentally. The smart pioneers unloaded their weapons and stored them in their wagons.

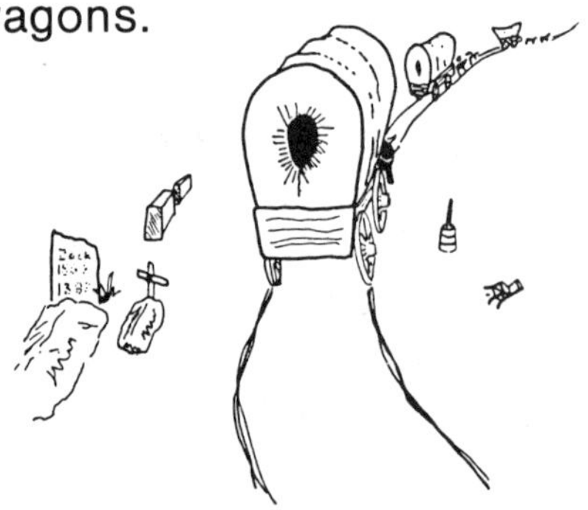

The wagons rumble along the trail which now follows the north side of the Kansas River. The wagon train comes to another river crossing, the Little Vermillion. Since this was a hard crossing, the pioneers were glad to see a bridge across the river. It was a toll bridge, operated by a Pottawatomie Indian, Louis Vieux.

Louis Vieux

Louis Vieux and several members of his family are buried in a little cemetery on the east side of the river.

Now swing the wagons north. (The trail follows the route of Kansas highway 99 for some distance.) The pioneers are now entering the area where they would see their first plains Indians—some hunting parties of Pawnee or a Sioux war party.

The pioneers, particularly the women, are frightened by the Indians. But the fact is, if the travelers stay on the trail and stick together, they will have little trouble with the Indians. If a person is foolish enough to wander off into the prairie alone —well, hard telling what would happen to that fool.

Up ahead lies another river to cross, the Big Blue River. But near the crossing is an excellent camp site, Alcove Springs. The pioneers will probably spend several days in camp here.

In the spring of 1846 a wagon train from Illinois camped at Alcove Spring. This marker tells the story of Sarah Keyes, aged 70, who was a member of that train. She died and was buried here while the wagon train was in camp.

Evening camp, especially in a nice spot like Alcove Springs, was the best time of the day. While mother prepared supper, the kids explored the campground. Dad tended the animals and then sat down to chat with the other men.

"Supper is ready," Mother called. The family gathered around the friendly campfire to eat fresh bread, fresh butter and milk (sure glad we brought along the old milk cow), fried meat, vegetables and a fragrant pie baked from berries gathered from bushes down by the river.

Covered Wagon Camp Ground

After supper the fun began. Some people sat around the campfires and talked. Folks from other wagon trains dropped by for a visit. Young people got out their musical instruments, and soon they were dancing on a level piece of prairie.

One Oregon-bound pioneer remembered that life at the campground was just like life in his village back east. At one end of the camp a young man and a young lady were being married by a preacher. From a nearby wagon came the cry of a newborn baby. And out on the prairie men and women attended the funeral of an old gentleman who had died that day.

Yes, life went on in the wagon train, just as though the pioneers were back home in Illinois or Missouri.

During their first three weeks on the trail the pioneers faced just about every problem they would meet in the next four months —terrible weather, bugs, muddy roads, clouds of choking dust, bad water, Indians, disease and accidents.

By this time many pioneers would have given up and turned around. Ask a discouraged fellow why he was returning to the East and he would probably say, "Because I've seen the elephant." This meant that he had endured enough hardships —broken wagon wheels, sick children, stubborn oxen, and muddy trails. He and his family were ready to go back home. They had "seen the elephant."

For the covered wagon pioneers who were determined to keep going to Oregon, there were many long miles ahead of them. They would face many obstacles; endure many hardships; and share in great adventures.

Ahead of them lay the land of their dreams —Oregon. And here they and their children would build their futures in a new country.

"These covered wagon pioneers are very important people. They prepared the way for thousands of families who crossed Kansas on their way to Oregon."

Chapter Seventeen
Trails West

The Forty-Niners

In 1849 gold was discovered in California. News of the discovery reached the East, and thousands of men decided to go to California and "strike it rich."

These gold-seekers called themselves "forty-niners." Among the "forty-niners" were old men and young men, rich and poor. There were also women in the army of persons who rushed west to California.

They streamed to the towns along the Missouri River where they could prepare to "jump off" for California. There were probably about 100,000 men, women and children who followed the California trail across eastern Kansas. This was the same trail that the Oregon emigrants had followed just a few years earlier. But now that trail had a new name—the California trail!

Among the thousands of forty-niners who streamed into Independence, Missouri, was George Winslow of Newton, Massachusetts. Leaving behind a good job, his wife and two little boys, George joined twenty-four of his friends for the trip to California. All of these young men had caught "gold fever."

George and his friends traveled by railroad and steamboat to Independence. After they arrived in Independence they bought wagons and mules. (Remember: pioneers who were in a hurry used mules or horses to pull their wagons. Oxen were too slow for these forty-niners.)

They pulled out of Independence on May 14, 1849. Like most of the forty-niners, these young men from Massachusetts knew very little about traveling the prairie trail. They had all kinds of difficulties. Their wagons broke down; their mules ran off. But the biggest problem was the weather. It rained constantly. Several times the men were soaked to the skin, and after one storm George became very ill.

The men made camp and put George to bed. They helped him the best they could, and after a few days George seemed to get better. So the wagon train hurried on, only to run into another storm. Again George became ill. His friends made him comfortable in a wagon and continued along the trail.

Just after they crossed the Kansas-Nebraska border (of course, in 1849 there was no border), George grew much worse. They made camp and shortly before dawn George died. His friends buried him by the trail, held a brief funeral service, and hurried west on the trail to California.

George Winslow's grave is located just north of Fairbury, Nebraska, a few miles from Kansas. As you walk to the grave, you will see the ruts left by the thousands of wagons which passed over the trail of the forty-niners.

The Pike's Peakers

In 1858 another group of gold-seekers poured across Kansas. This time gold had been discovered in Colorado. Since the gold mines were near Pike's Peak, these persons who hunted gold were known as "Pike's Peakers."

Many of those who participated in the rush to Colorado traveled across Kansas. They left the towns along the Missouri River with high hopes. On the canvas tops of their wagons many wrote the phrase, "Pike's Peak or Bust!"

This wonderful photograph was taken in St. Joseph, Missouri, in 1858 or 1859. The man is leaving for Colorado. Study the photograph carefully and answer these questions:
1. What kind of wagon is the man using?
2. Why is he using mules to pull the wagon?
3. What do you suppose he is carrying in the wagon?
4. See the woman standing by the wagon? Let's suppose that this lady is the Pike's Peaker's wife. What do you think she is telling her husband? What do you think he would say to her in return?

This is a "wind wagon."

There were interesting sights to be seen on the Colorado gold rush trail. Several men built what they called "wind wagons."

The "wind wagons" worked quite well. There was no shortage of wind to worry about—not on the Kansas prairie, that's for sure.

Then there were the men who walked all the way to Colorado. They pushed wheelbarrows loaded with food and equipment. Quite a load to push across the plains!

Women followed the trail, too. They usually wore pants and shirts—long dresses weren't suitable for traveling the trail.

The first Pike's Peakers followed the Oregon-California trail up through Nebraska. But somebody figured that the men would save miles—and time—by following a trail straight across Kansas. The last part of the trail lay along the Smoky Hill River.

The plan looked fine on the map. But the gold-seekers who selected this trail were soon disappointed. There was very little water along the trail and not much grass for their animals. The worst thing was, however, that the trail ran through country hostile

Indians still controlled. Those who followed the Smoky Hill trail suffered terribly; many died on the prairie.

But even those who got to Colorado quickly and easily didn't always "strike it rich." No, gold was hard to find, and many of the Pike's Peakers gave up and returned home. This drawing shows the outfit of a disappointed Pike's Peaker.

Every year more and more people went west. Many of them found the West to be a land of opportunity. Some became town-builders. Others worked in the mines. Many were interested in becoming farmers and ranchers. And of course there were many Army posts scattered over the plains and mountains.

The point is this: these people needed supplies from the East. Miners needed equipment. Town merchants needed goods to sell. The soldiers had to have food, clothing and ammunition.

Let's talk now about how the needed supplies crossed the plains.

The Freighters

To supply the things the western settlers needed, freight lines were established which ran from Kansas towns on the Missouri River west across the plains. At towns, such as Atchison, big steamboats unloaded their cargoes. The boxes, bags, barrels and bales were loaded into huge freight wagons for the trip west.

The wagons were drawn by eight or ten oxen. Experienced bullwhackers directed the wagons; many of them had learned their business on the Santa Fe trail. They cracked their long whips over the backs of the oxen and the wagons rolled along the trails. Weeks later they rumbled into towns, mining camps and Army posts with the needed supplies.

A freight train crossing a Kansas River.

Freighting was a big business. In 1858, for example, Atchison was a very busy starting point for freighters. Twenty-four freight "trains" pulled out of Atchison that year. In these trains there were 775 wagons carrying almost four million pounds of freight. The wagons were pulled by 7,963 oxen and 1,286 mules. There were 1,114 men handling the wagons and animals.

Some of the freighting outfits were large outfits with many wagons and many employees. Sometimes there was just one man with his own wagon who worked in the business.

And the freighters were willing to carry any cargo, so long as they made money. One freighter learned that the Colorado miners were having trouble with mice and rats. This smart fellow rounded up all the stray cats he could find —about two hundred of them. He crossed the plains with his howling, yowling cargo. In the mining camps he sold each cat for ten dollars. He made a good profit from his unusual cargo.

Freighters camped along the trail.

The Pony Express

Fast mail service, which the people in California and other parts of the West demanded, was provided by the famous Pony Express.

The Pony Express line started in St. Joseph, Missouri, crossed eastern Kansas into Nebraska, and finally delivered the mail in California. The trail was nearly 2,000 miles long.

The Pony Express began operating in 1860. Sixty young men were hired to carry the mail. Each received a salary of $50 per month, plus board and room. The riders were small men. None weighed more than 130 pounds.

Each rider covered a forty-five mile section of the trail. At the end of his forty-five mile stretch, the rider handed the leather **mochila**, which contained the mail, to the next rider. Then he waited for the next rider, coming from the opposite direction, who would hand him his mochila, and the rider would retrace the forty-five mile route.

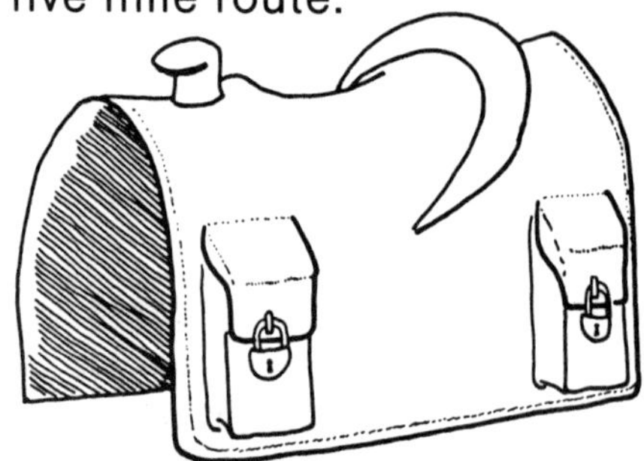

Pony Express stations were set up about every fifteen miles. The riders changed horses at the stations. In Marysville a Pony Express barn stands, and east of Hanover a Pony Express station has been preserved.

The Hollenberg Pony Express Station.

How thrilling it must have been to see the Pony Express rider gallop up to the station! He pulls his sweating pony to a stop and leaps to the ground. He throws his mochila on a fresh horse that is waiting for him. Then he leaps into the saddle and dashes off down the trail. All of this action occurred within a minute or two.

How much did it cost to send a letter by the Pony Express? For a letter that weighed one-half ounce —and that is not a very big letter—the charge was between $2.50 and $5.00.

The Pony Express lasted for only about eighteen months. But the Pony Express is an important part of our past. Certainly we should remember the young men who carried the mail. There was James Moore who rode 280 miles in fourteen hours. There was fourteen year old Bill Cody (later to be known as "Buffalo Bill" Cody) who in an emergency carried the mail 230 miles. And there was Jack Keetley who, on a bet, rode 340 miles in 31 hours —without a single stop to rest.

It took ten days to carry the mail from Missouri to California. No matter the weather—rain, snow, mud or dust—the riders carried the mail. Only one pouch of letters was lost—a remarkable record.

The telegraph wire, strung across the plains, put the Pony Express out of business. The metal wires carried messages much faster than the gallant men and horses of the Pony Express.

Stagecoaches: For People in a Hurry!

In the late 1850's no one wanted to cross the plains in ox-drawn wagons. No, sir! People were in a hurry! They purchased tickets in the new stagecoaches that dashed over the land.

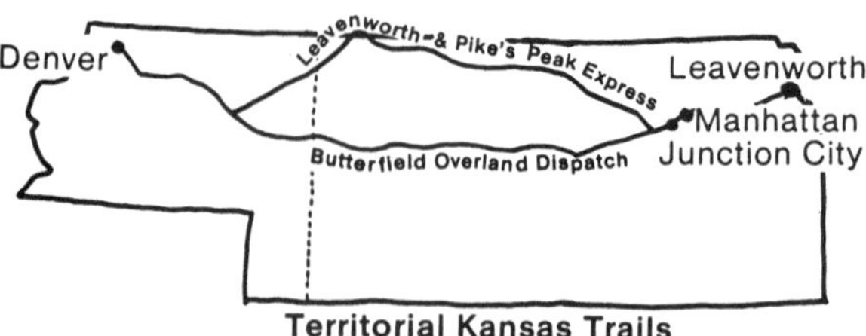

Territorial Kansas Trails

There were two important stage lines in Kansas: the Leavenworth and Pike's Peak Express company; and the Butterfield Overland Dispatch.

The Leavenworth and Pike's Peak Express Company laid out a route across northern Kansas, as you can see on the map. Station Thirteen on this stage line stood in what is today the town of Kirwin, Phillips County.

The Butterfield line was established by David Butterfield.

David Butterfield.

His coaches followed the regular stage road to Fort Riley. Then they headed up the valley of the Smoky Hill River to Denver.

Historical markers, which carry the letters BOD, mark the trail of the famous Butterfield stage line across Kansas.

This marker stands at the site of Monument station on the Butterfield stage line. See the beautiful Monument Rocks in the background?

The Smoky Hill trail was a tough road—the Pike's Peakers had discovered that fact. And the stage drivers had no easier time.

Many coaches were attacked by Indians.

The Army provided armed escorts for the stages during particularly dangerous periods.

Stagecoaches usually had inside seating for nine passengers. Another four or five could ride on top of the coach, but these seats were uncomfortable and dangerous.

There is only one word to describe a stagecoach ride—**rough!** The coach bounced and swayed because of the rough trail. Passengers were thrown from one side of the coach to the other. It was said that if a passenger managed to

live through the first day of his trip, he or she had a pretty good chance of making it to the end of the line.

Passengers were not happy with the food served at the stage stations either. At one station dinner consisted of a few pieces of greasy meat, a chunk of week-old bread and a cup of milk —filled with dead flies! Each station charged the passengers for their meals, and this cost was in addition to the $100 to $200 fare they had paid.

Stage drivers were colorful characters. They were skilled and competent drivers who knew how to handle horses and mules. It took a good driver to keep a stage on schedule. Usually they averaged about nine miles an hour through all kinds of weather and over all kinds of roads.

For many years stagecoaches operated in Kansas. Even after the first railroads were built, stages continued to run to towns which did not have railroad connections. The stagecoach, with its driver and fine teams of mules or horses, was an important and long-remembered part of your Kansas pioneer heritage.

A stage coach leaving Atchison

A stage coach at Dodge City

UNIT SIX:
THE PRAIRIE PIONEERS

KANSAS BUGLE

ISS. No. 5 Vol. IV AUG 1854

YOUR FUTURE IS IN KANSAS

KANSAS TERRITORY FORMED

New towns of "Promise" in Kansas

"Fine" Land for farmers says Scout

Railroad Sure to Come!

DESERT IS CONQUERED

"Tell your friends and relatives in the East and in Europe about Kansas"

"Yes, tell them to come to Kansas . . . the LAND OF THE PIONEERS."

Chapter Eighteen
Town-Builders

Congress established Kansas Territory in 1854 and opened the land to settlers. Many of the first persons to come to Kansas were town-builders.

These people knew that there was money to be made in building new towns. They also knew that the country needed towns.

A few crooked town-builders were included in the ranks of the pioneers. These rascals had no intention of building real towns. They printed up beautiful maps and pictures of their towns and passed these advertisements around in the East. People bought lots in the town and expected to make money from their investments.

Here is an advertisement prepared by the promoters of New Babylon.

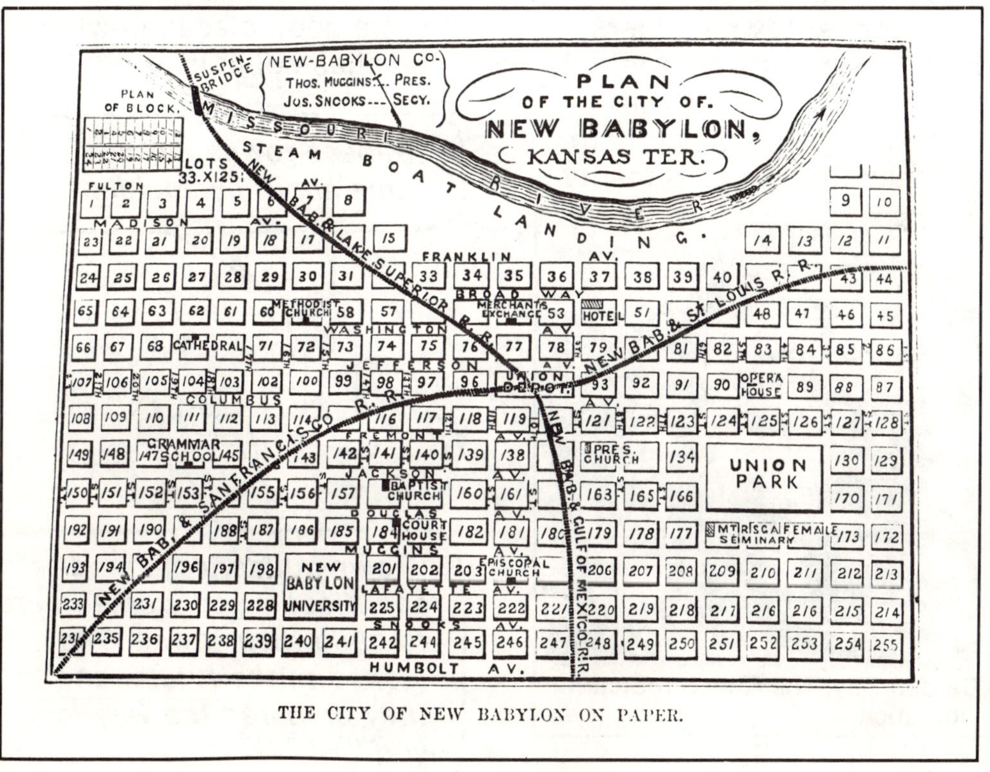

THE CITY OF NEW BABYLON ON PAPER.

Those who bought lots in New Babylon were in for a shock when they came to see the town. Here is how the town really looked!

THE CITY OF NEW BABYLON IN FACT.

What did the town-builders think about as they planned their towns?

1. They had to find a good location for their town.
2. They wanted to attract business and industries to the town.
3. They wanted to establish an orderly community with good government.
4. They wanted their towns to be good places in which families could live.

Most of the town-builders were honest workers. They wanted to build towns that would grow and prosper. The pioneer town-builders had a vision of what their towns would one day be like—and they worked hard to make that vision a reality.

Garden City: The New Streetcar in Operation.

Kansas City, like every Kansas community, is a monument to our pioneer town-builders.

Atchison was a Missouri River town. Steamboats brought people and cargoes to Atchison's wharves, and the town became an important starting point for overland freighters. Atchison was established by men from Missouri who wanted to make Kansas slave territory.

This marker tells about the founding of Manhattan. Town-builders from Ohio came up the Kansas River by steamboat. They liked this spot, but discovered that another town company had already claimed the site for a town they had named Boston. The new arrivals said they would settle here if the name of the town was changed to Manhattan—which was done. Manhattan was a "free state" town.

Eli Thayer

Eli Thayer, of Worcester, Massachusetts, was a very important Kansas town-builder. He organized a number of anti-slavery town companies which came to Kansas, including the group which founded Lawrence.

Cyrus Holliday

Cyrus K. Holliday was another Kansas town-builder. He came to Kansas in 1854 from Pennsylvania where he operated a small railroad. After arriving in Kansas Mr. Holliday wrote the following to his wife: "I am now thirty miles above Lawrence on the Kansas River, assisting in starting a new town. We are just about in the central portion of the settled territory and with perhaps the best landing and the most eligible site for a city in the entire country . . ." What "new town" do you think Mr. Holliday was helping establish? The town was Topeka. Yes, Holliday was a member of the Topeka Town Company which laid out the future capital of Kansas. Later Mr. Holliday helped set up the Atchison, Topeka and Santa Fe Railroad. He was a very significant person in the development of Kansas.

I am reading the interesting historical marker which stands in downtown Girard, Crawford County. According to the marker, Dr. Charles Strong, from Girard, Pennsylvania, shot a deer on this spot. (See the statue of the deer?) The year was 1868, and Mr. Girard, as secretary of a town company, was looking for a good town site. He selected this spot for the town which was named for his home in Penn sylvania. Girard grew rapidly. In 1870 the town had 140 buildings, including five hotels, eight saloons, six grocery stores, five dry goods stores, two hardware stores, two furniture stores, a drug store, a newspaper and seventy-five homes. The railroad arrived that year, and Girard's future was assured.

In 1877 a very interesting town was laid out in Graham County. The town's name was Nicodemus, and it was settled by Black families, most of whom came from Kentucky. Two years later the prairie town had thirty-five houses, two churches and one store. Most of the buildings were made of sod. I am standing in front of the African Methodist Church which was built in 1885. Nicodemus was named for an escaped Black slave, whose story all the Black people knew by heart.

NICODEMUS,
THE GATE CITY OF GRAHAM COUNTY
has had no unhealthy boom, but has kept steady pace with the development of the surrounding country.
Nicodemus has excellent water, enterprising citizens, good schools, churches and is surrounded by farming lands that surpass any in the beautiful South Solomon Valley.
If you are looking for safe investments, sure profits and home where the people are wide awake take advantage of the cheap rates

All Colored People
THAT WANT TO
GO TO KANSAS,
On September 5th, 1877,
Can do so for $5.00

IMMIGRATION.

WHEREAS, We, the colored people of Lexington, Ky., knowing that there is an abundance of choice lands now belonging to the Government, have assembled ourselves together for the purpose of locating on said lands. Therefore,

BE IT RESOLVED, That we do now organize ourselves into a Colony, as follows:— Any person wishing to become a member of this Colony can do so by paying the sum of

Ho for Kansas!
Brethren, Friends, & Fellow Citizens:
I feel thankful to inform you that the
REAL ESTATE
AND
Homestead Association,
Will Leave Here the
15th of April, 1878,
In pursuit of Homes in the Southwestern Lands of America, at Transportation Rates, cheaper than ever was known before.
For full information inquire of
Benj. Singleton, better known as old Pap,
NO. 5 NORTH FRONT STREET.
Beware of Speculators and Adventurers, as it is a dangerous thing to fall in their hands.
Nashville, Tenn., March 18, 1878.

Articles and posters, such as these, encouraged Black families to leave the South and come to Kansas. In 1880 nearly five hundred Black pioneers lived in Graham County.

The Stockton "hotel."

McKanna homestead marker

In 1878 Mary S. McKanna homesteaded in Rooks County. Later the town of Stockton was built on her land. The town was located in ranch country. Originally it was called Stocktown. Right next to this marker stands a log building which was the hotel where visiting cattlemen stayed.

"What do you know about the town where you live or where you go to school? Can you answer these questions?

1. Who were the town-builders who founded this town?
2. Why did they build a town here?
3. How did the town get its name?

"Go to your People Bank. There are adults in your town who can help you find the answers for these questions."

Optimistic Kansas town-builders believed that steamboats could be used on other rivers. This steamboat, built in Pittsburgh, Pennsylvania, was brought to Kansas to be used on the Kansas River. But most of the time the Kansas River—as well as the other rivers in Kansas—did not have enough water to float steamboats.

"Here is another question for which you need to find an answer: Why did the town-builders select this spot for your town?"

Leavenworth in 1857.

Most of the first towns in Kansas were built along the Missouri River. Steamboats docked at the towns, bringing both people and cargoes. A town had to have good transportation, and in the 1850's town-builders wanted their towns to be along navigable rivers.

Railroad Depot

The town-builders were not discouraged, however. They knew that railroads would soon be built in Kansas. And they worked hard to get railroads built to their towns. The railroad was every town's key to success!

Salina ferry marker

Salina grew up where a ferry was used by pioneers to cross the Smoky Hill River. It was an excellent town site. Everyone who lived in the area came to use the ferry. And they would visit the shops and stores in the town while they were here.

Kansas mill

There was another reason for building a town near a river. Town-builders knew that dams could be built across the rivers and water power used for factories and mills. Imagine that! The pioneers thought about energy too! Mills were very important industries in the pioneer towns. Farmers brought their grain to mills to be made into feed and flour. They were the towns' first major industry.

The ferry at Lawrence carried wagons across the Kansas River

Empire City — boomtown — main street

Just as today, pioneeer town-builders knew that a town had to have a supply of cheap fuel. Where coal was discovered, towns immediately appeared. This is the "boom town" of Empire City, a mining town in southeastern Kansas.

Coal, a valuable energy source, helped Kansas grow economically and industrially. This coal mine was near Pittsburg.

This is Croweburg, in Crawford County, a town where the coal miners and their families lived.

Mining pit and shovel

Fort Scott is another kind of town. It grew up around a famous Army post some of whose historic buildings stand today—waiting for your visit!

"Do these stories and pictures help you understand why your town was built where it is?"

"Now let's take a walk down Main Street of a pioneer town. Let's see what is going on."

The business place in a pioneer Kansas town was the railroad depot. Everyone in town came down to watch the trains come and go. For the young people in town it was a particularly exciting place.

Another very important business stood near the depot—the grain elevator. Farmers who lived near the town sold their grain at the

elevator. The money they received for their crops was spent in the town's stores. Pioneer towns depended upon the farmers' business —just as do modern Kansas towns.

Now, take a look down Main Street. One of the important pioneer businesses you'll see is the newspaper. This is the building where the Oskaloosa **Independent**, a pioneer Kansas newspaper, was printed.

The Oskaloosa Independent Building

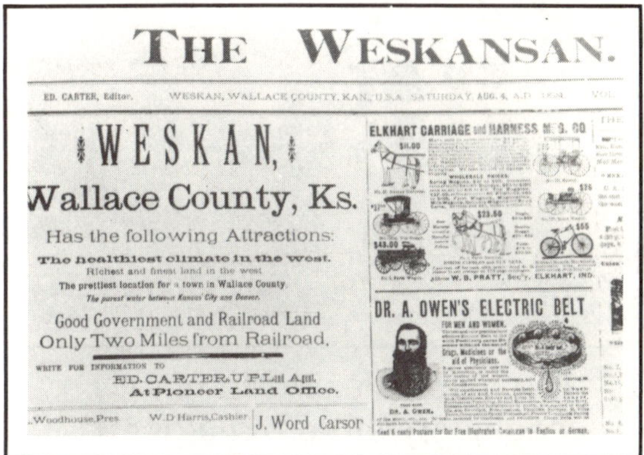

THE WESKANSAN.

ED. CARTER, Editor. WESKAN, WALLACE COUNTY, KAN., U.S.A. SATURDAY, AUG. 4, A.D.

WESKAN,

Wallace County, Ks.

Has the following Attractions:

The healthiest climate in the west.

Richest and finest land in the west

The prettiest location for a town in Wallace County

The purest water between Kansas City and Denver.

Good Government and Railroad Land

Only Two Miles from Railroad.

WRITE FOR INFORMATION TO

ED. CARTER, U.P. Land Agent,

At Pioneer Land Office.

Woodhouse, Pres. W.D Harris, Cashier | J. Word Carsor

ELKHART CARRIAGE and HARNESS MFG. CO

W. B. PRATT, Sec'y, ELKHART, IND.

DR. A. OWEN'S ELECTRIC BELT

FOR MEN AND WOMEN.

DR. A. OWEN.

Newspapers were very important to the pioneer communities. They spread the good news about the town and the county and urged people come live in Kansas.

A town would have several "general" stores where one could purchase everything from clothing to groceries.

The hardware and farm machinery store did a good business in pioneer towns. While Pa was buying a new plow or new wagon in this Abilene store, Ma could go next door and stock up on items she needed from the drug store.

Settlers had a great deal of business to do at the local bank—from setting up checking accounts to borrowing money.

The local post office was located in the Carlton Bank. See the postman's wagon parked in front?

Suppose you came to town for a visit. You wanted to look over the country around the town—perhaps you wanted to buy some farm land. You went to the livery stable and rented a horse and buggy.

And if your horses needed new shoes, you took them to one of the blacksmiths in town.

A town had to have a hotel or two. One of the first hotels in Dighton was this sod building. The two customers appear to be pleased with their accommodations.

And if you wanted to know what was going on in Englewood, you stopped in at the local barber shop. Men gathered here to swap stories and to visit. Once in a while they even got a shave or a haircut.

This marker in Garden City tells about a business that was very, very important to a pioneer town. The United States Land Office stood on this spot. Only a few Kansas towns had Land Offices to which settlers came by the hundreds to file their land claims.

Here is the crowd that showed up when the Garden City Land Office opened for business in 1883.

A town that had the county seat was a very fortunate town. That is why the town-builders fought like cats and dogs to get the county court house. Settlers came to the county seat on all kinds of business, and of course they made purchases in the stores while they were in town. This marker in Johnson City reminds the residents of the modern town how important the school and the county court house were in the development of the town.

There was one sure sign that your town was growing and prospering—that was when a streetcar line was built on Main Street, like this one in Cottonwood Falls. A ride in a handsome streetcar convinced you that you lived in a real "metropolis."

Yes, if everything went according to the town-builders' plans, Main Street was soon lined with thriving businesses and, as here in Wichita, a busy land office.

The town-builders worked hard to let people know about their towns. They used all kinds of advertisements, including posters like this one. What town did this poster promote?

"Hard work, money and determination went into building successful towns in Kansas.

"And in order for towns to be good places in which to live, the town-builders set up local governments. Men and women elected to public offices provided the services the people needed."

One of the most important services was that provided by the fire department. Most of the buildings in the new towns were made of wood. Firemen protected the town against disastrous fires.

Policemen were needed to enforce local laws. In many Kansas towns there was a problem with the teen-agers who raced up and down main street in their horse-drawn buggies. Weren't teen-agers terrible?

Here are Mr. and Mrs. Salter. Mrs. Susanna Salter was elected mayor of Argonia in 1887. She was the first woman mayor in Kansas.

It was not unusual for women to be elected to public office in Kansas towns.

Mothers and fathers wanted good schools for their children. This Scott City school, like every Kansas school, prepared the citizens of the future.

The pioneer churches may not have had handsome buildings, but the churches, including this Wichita church, helped people in the town work together and to understand what they wanted the town to be.

Pioneer Wichita church

Many community activities were held in the Opera House. As I visited the old Opera House in Grainfield, a wonderful lady stopped to tell me that her graduation exercises had been held in the building. She told me about the traveling theatrical troupes which put on plays in the Opera House, and about the parties and meetings that were held there too.

Men attended meetings of the local lodges. The lodges provided insurance for the men; and when a member died, the lodge provided care for his widow and children.

Wonderful parades were held on the Fourth of July.

Robert Manley and Opera House

Yes, Pioneer Kansas towns were busy places!

Fourth of July parade

Lodge members

There would be speeches after the parade, followed by games in the afternoon and fireworks in the evening.

Summer afternoons the folks went out to the ball park to see the local team do battle with rival teams from other towns.

Some Kansas school oraganized teams to play the new sport known as "foot ball." Townspeople thought the game was pretty rough; some schools prohibited the boys from playing the sport. But the boys enjoyed "knocking heads" on the gridiron.

Everyone in town agreed, however, that a high point of the year came when the circus arrived in town.

Yes, there were exciting things to do in Kansas' pioneer towns. People were proud to live in "wide-awake" and growing towns.

Over the years, however, towns changed. The automobile came to town, and many blacksmith shops, harness shops and wagon shops went out of business. People were getting rid of their horses and buying the new "horseless carriages."

Grandpa remembered the time the streets of Kinsley were filled with horses and buggies. He lived to see the automobiles running around the town.

What do you think will happen to the town in which you live in the next fifty years? In the year 2025 how will people travel? What kinds of stores will be on Main Street? What industries will be located in the town? What kind of schools will your children attend?

Ness City today

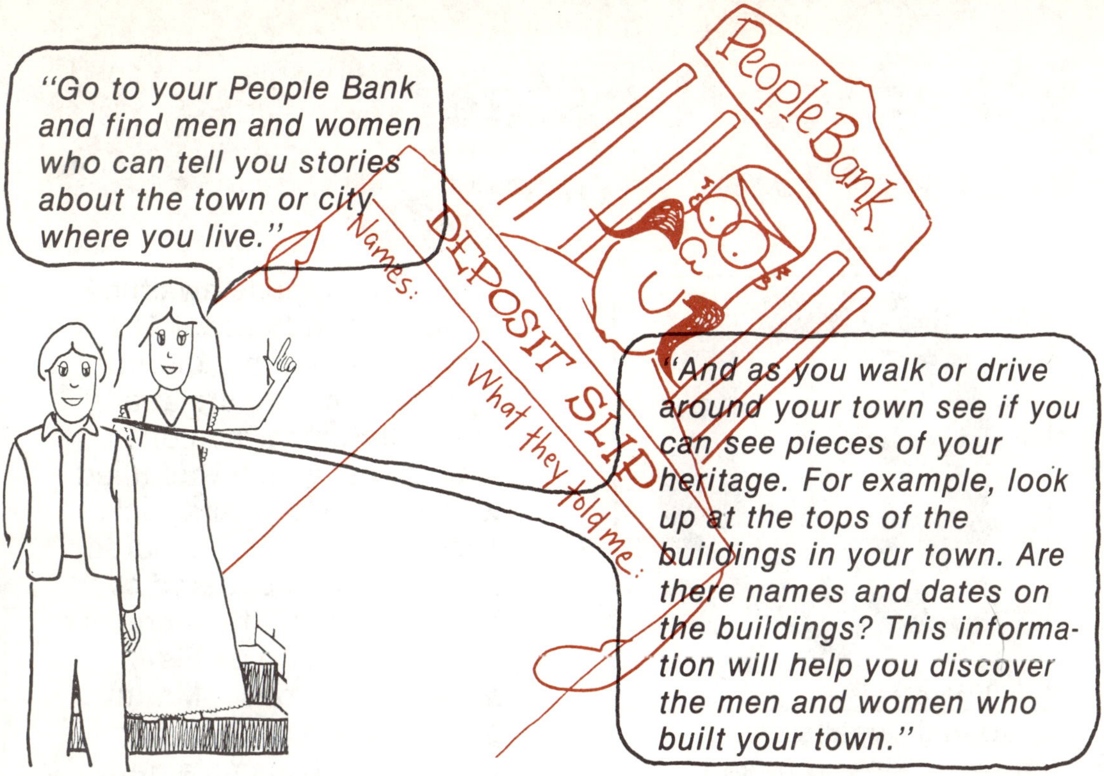

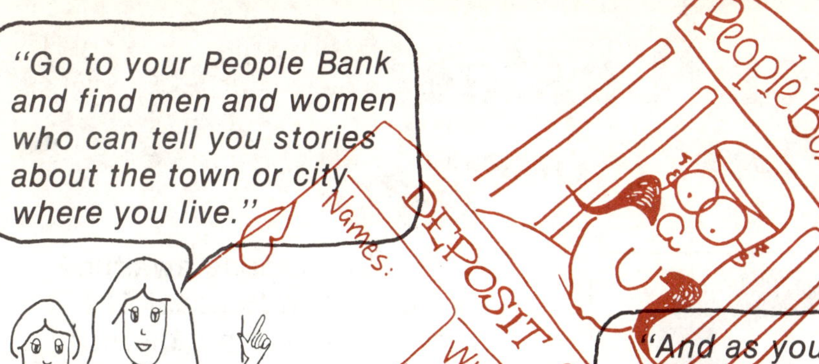

"And as you walk or drive around your town see if you can see pieces of your heritage. For example, look up at the tops of the buildings in your town. Are there names and dates on the buildings? This information will help you discover the men and women who built your town."

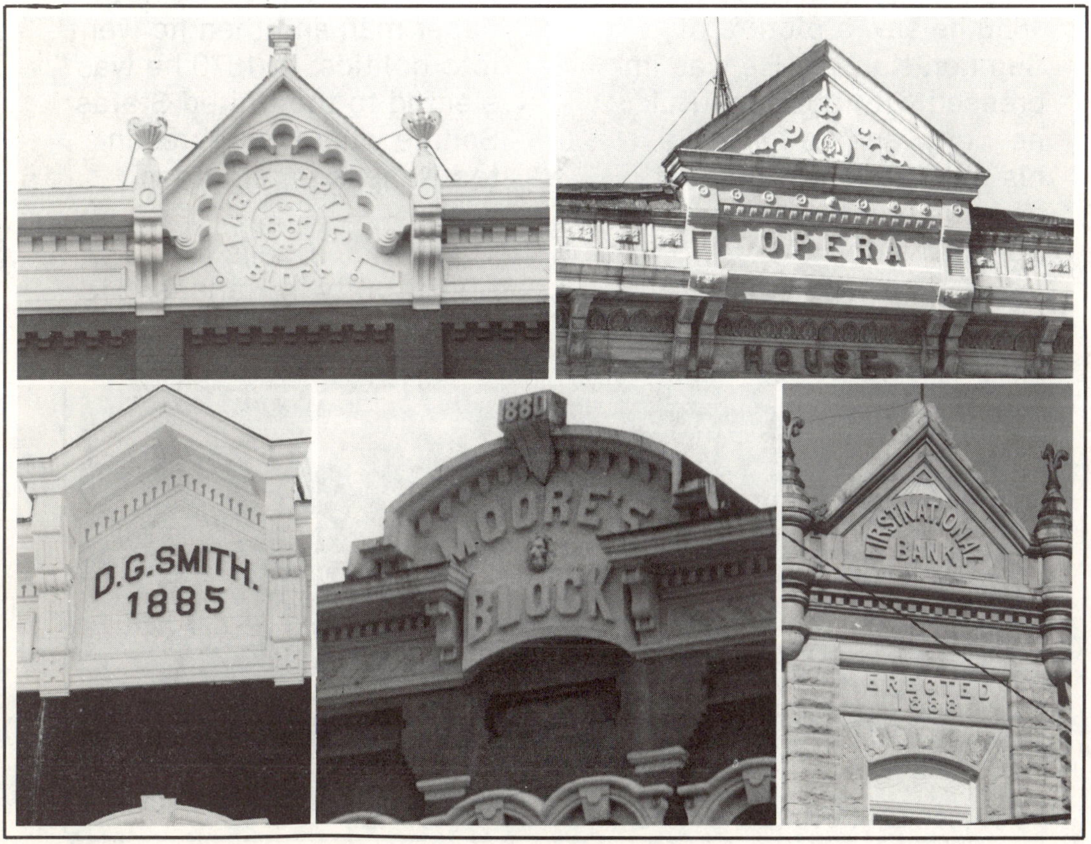

Chapter Nineteen
Political Pioneers

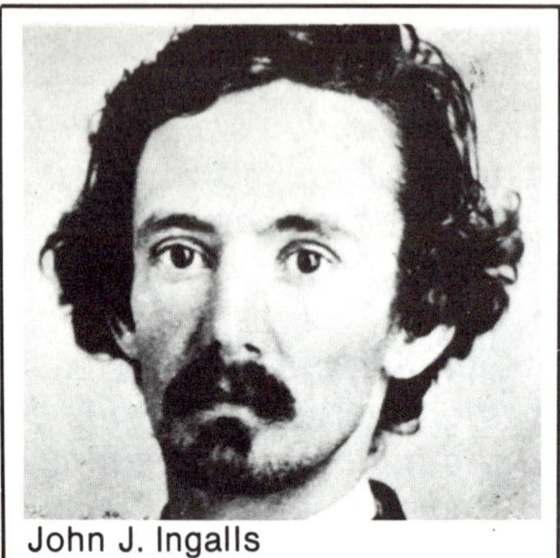
John J. Ingalls

John J. Ingalls was a native of Massachusetts. In 1858 he saw a picture of Sumner, Kansas. He was impressed with the beautiful, new city, and he made up his mind to leave the East and come to Kansas.

What a surprise awaited Mr. Ingalls in Kansas! The real city of Sumner did not resemble the picture at all! The real Sumner had one main street which was filled with tree stumps and rocks. There were several hundred crude shacks scattered over the hills—and little more.

After he got over his anger and surprise, Mr. Ingalls decided to remain in Kansas. He became a newspaper man and then he went into politics. In 1878 he was elected to the United States Senate where he represented Kansas for eighteen years.

John J. Ingalls found opportunity in Kansas. He

The picture of Sumner, Kansas, which Mr. Ingalls saw.

was an important political pioneer.

Kansas Territory

Congress, you remember, formed Kansas Territory in 1854. Crowds of people rushed into the new territory. These eager settlers wanted to get control of the best town sites and to lay claim to the best lands. There was no organized government as yet in Kansas; confusion and disorder were everywhere.

Many of the first settlers came from the nearby state of Missouri. They wanted Kansas to be a slave territory. And there were groups of anti-slave people who came to Kansas. Of course, these people, with their opposing views on slavery, did not get along very well.

The first capital of Kansas Territory.

Andrew H. Reeder was named the first governor of Kansas Territory by the Federal government, and he asked the legislators to meet for the first time in the town of Pawnee. A large stone warehouse in Pawnee was turned into the "capitol," and the representatives gathered on the first floor, while the senators met on the second floor of the building.

For several years the Territorial Legislature met in this building in Lecompton. These sessions were usually controlled by the pro-slave group. In 1858 the legislators wrote the so-called "Lecompton Constitution" for the State of Kansas, which allowed slavery. The voters of Kansas turned down that constitution.

Most of the men who attended this 1855 session of the legislature favored slavery. And they did not want Pawnee to be the capital of Kansas Territory. After being in session for only a few days, the legislators voted to move to the Shawnee Mission.

Pawnee was no longer the capital of Kansas Territory—and the fight between the anti-slavery and pro-slavery settlers had begun.

In the East organizations were formed to send anti-slavery settlers to Kansas Territory. In 1856 a group of people from Connecticut decided to come to Kansas. Henry Ward Beecher, a famous anti-slavery minister, gave the settlers Bibles and money to purchase guns.

These anti-slavery colonists laid out the town of Wabaunsee, and they built a handsome church. The church, which still stands, is known as the Beecher Bible and Rifle Church.

The Beecher Bible and Rifle Church in Wabaunsee.

About this time a man arrived in Kansas who became a leader of the anti-slavery settlers. His name was John Brown, and he, with several of his sons, settled near Osawatomie.

John Brown

Brown was convinced that the supporters of slavery had to be defeated —crushed—and driven from Kansas. In 1856 he and his sons killed five pro-slavery settlers. After this event fighting swept across Kansas.

A few years later, a gang of pro-slavery men rounded up eleven free state settlers. The captives were lined up and shot. Five were killed; five were wounded; only one escaped without injury.

The Marais Des Cygnes Massacre.

It is no wonder Kansas came to be known as "Bleeding Kansas." But you must remember that much of the conflict was not because of slavery. No. In every frontier area there was always disorder and fighting. Kansans fought over land claims. There were neighborhood quarrels between families. And the newspapers of the day exaggerated the stories of bloodshed, too. Men who were running for political office also might exaggerate stories in order to obtain votes.

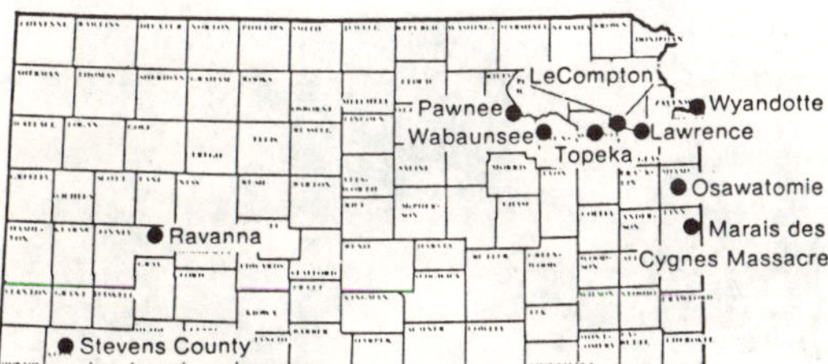

On January 29, 1861, Kansas became a state. A few months later the Civil War began, and thousands of Kansans went off to war.

The war came to eastern Kansas when bands of bold Southern soldiers dashed across the land, killing, burning and looting as they went. One band of raiders took over the town of Lawrence. Much of the town was burned and more than 150 persons were killed.

Kansas soldiers in the Civil War.

In the Lawrence cemetery are many tombstones, such as this, which mark the graves of persons killed in the Lawrence raid.

To get even with the Confederates from Missouri who raided eastern Kansas, Union men who lived in Kansas formed raiding parties and attacked Missouri farms and towns. These Union raiders were often known as "jayhawkers."

John J. Ingalls, whom you met at the beginning of this chapter, thought up the motto of the State of Kansas: "To the stars through difficulties."

There is no better description of life in pioneer Kansas. These were difficult days for Kansas, but political pioneers were hard at work preparing for a better future.

County Government

The Territorial law-makers laid out counties and set up elections at which county officials were elected. The men who were elected to the office had many jobs to do. And sometimes they did not receive pay for their work. In Chase County, for example, county officials did not receive salaries. According to one resident of the county, the people of Chase County were willing to do without the services of county officers rather than "place themselves under burdensome taxation."

The Chase County Courthouse in Cottonwood Falls is a beautiful monument to this county's political pioneers.

County officers saw to it that roads and bridges were built and taken care of. They organized schools and collected taxes to support the schools.

County officials took care of poor people, and the county sheriff enforced the law. Law and order was handled by county judges.

The Hodgeman County Courthouse in Jetmore.

When a county was formed by the legislature the big question was which town in the county would get the county seat. The county seat town almost always prospered, so in many Kansas counties towns fought —and shed blood— over the location of the county seat.

A county seat "war" was fought in Stevens County between the towns of Hugoton and Woodsdale. Several times State troops were called in to stop the violence. In the end six men died in the fighting, including a well-known Kansas editor, Samuel Wood.

Samuel Wood, who died in the Stevens County "war."

In Garfield County the towns of Eminence and Ravenna quarreled over the county seat. In this case, however, neither town won. In fact Garfield County disappeared —it was absorbed by Finney County. Eminence died, and only piles of rubble mark the site of Ravenna.

The Ravanna School—then.

The Ravanna School—now.

The Ravanna Courthouse—then.

The Ravanna Courthouse—now.

"What do you know about the county where you live? Can you answer these questions?"

1. When was this county formed?
2. How did this county get its name?
3. Was there a fight in this county over the location of the county seat?
4. Who were the "political pioneers" in this county?

"Go to your People Bank and find adults who can help you answer these questions. You should learn all you can about the county where you live."

Republic County officials, 1886—some political pioneers!

City and Town Government

Don't forget that the new towns in Kansas needed governments, too. The residents in the new prairie towns elected officials whose job it was to establish law and order—not always an easy thing to do in some towns.

Plains, like every town, needed good government and good officials in office.

The town's officials quickly wrote laws for the town. Most of them were negative. Here are some examples:

No hogs running loose in the streets.
No racing teams in the streets.
No leaving teams unhitched in front of stores.
No dumping trash or garbage in the streets.
No shooting guns inside the city limits.

Many towns had ordinances which said baseball could not be played on Sunday. And there were laws against dancing on Sunday. Some towns set up a curfew. That is, after a certain time at night all young people had to be off the streets and in their homes.

Town officials also had laws concerning chimneys and stoves. They wanted to be sure that a poor chimney or an improperly installed stove did not start a fire that would burn down the whole town. Policemen in these towns spent most of their time watching for fires.

The elected officials of the cities and towns had many responsibilities. But in the spirit of the pioneers, they met these responsibilities and laid the foundation for a better future.

Meade, a pioneer town.

Charles Robinson was elected the first governor of Kansas. He belonged to the newly-formed Republican party.

State Government

On January 29, 1861, the President of the United States, James Buchanan, signed the bill which created the State of Kansas.

After four tries, Kansas' political pioneers wrote a constitution which both Congress and the people of Kansas would accept. It had been written at Wyandotte (now part of Kansas City) by a convention made up mostly of free state men. Kansas came into the Union, of course, as a free State.

Life was not easy in the new State of Kansas. Keep in mind that Kansas became a state just as the Civil War started. And the war had a tremendous impact upon the people of Kansas, as you know.

Worse yet, drought seared the land. Crops died and many families faced starvation because of the hard times. As one Kansas newspaper man wrote, "Bleeding Kansas" became "starving Kansas." And the second condition was nearly as bad as the first!

Little by little, however, conditions improved. Additions were built on to the capitol building in Topeka —a sign that Kansas was growing and expanding.

In this beautiful building the political leaders of the State deal with the problems which face all Kansans. And they prepare the way for the next generation of Kansans.

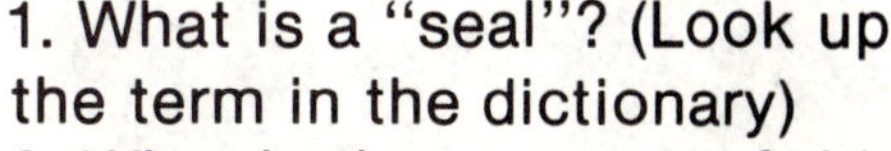

1. What is a "seal"? (Look up the term in the dictionary)
2. What is the purpose of this seal?
3. Why is the date, January 29, 1861, on the seal?
4. What is the meaning of the Latin phrase, "Ad Astra Per Aspera"?
5. What people and objects can you identify on the seal? What do these people and objects tell you about your pioneer heritage?

The State capitol in Topeka

SOME POLITICAL PIONEERS OF KANSAS

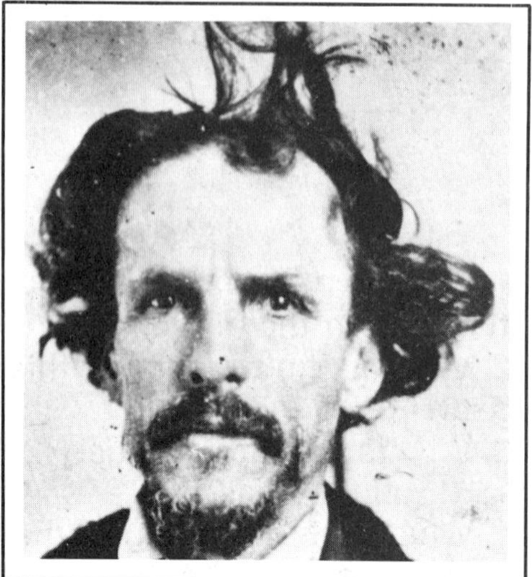

Jim Lane was a free state leader and the first United States Senator from Kansas. Lane was a fiery speaker and a fierce opponent of slavery.

Carry Nation was a leader in the anti-liquor and anti-saloon movement in Kansas. Prohibition, that is, making the production and sale of alcoholic beverages illegal, has been an issue in Kansas politics for years.

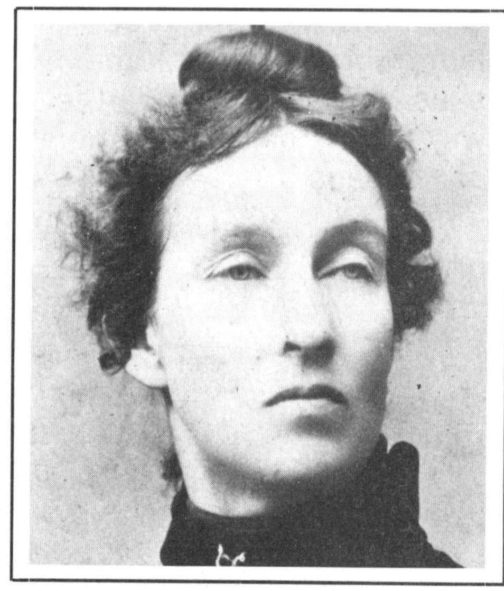

Mrs. Mary Lease was another important woman in Kansas politics. In the 1890's Kansas farmers were in serious economic difficulties. Mrs. Lease took the side of the farmers. She gave speeches all over Kansas arguing that the government should help the farmers. Mrs. Lease worked with the Populist, or People's, Party.

William Allen White was one of the most influential newspaper editors in Kansas—and in the entire United States. He was an editor of the Emporia **Gazette**. Mr. White was interested in effective, progressive government.

Arthur Capper was born in Garnett. At the age of 14 he went to work for a printer. A few years later he became a reporter, and then owner of a newspaper. Eventually he was a very successful publisher of farm newspapers. He served two terms as Governor of Kansas and five terms as United States Senator.

Alfred Landon (better known as Alf Landon) served as Governor from 1933 to 1937. In 1936 he was the candidate of the Republican Party for the office of President of the United States. Kansans respect Governor Landon for his honesty and dedication to good government.

Dwight Eisenhower spent his boyhood in Abilene. After graduating from the United States Military Academy at West Point, he had an outstanding career in the Army. During World War II he was commander of our armies in Europe. In 1952 he was elected President of the United States. In 1956 he was elected to a second term. Dwight Eisenhower is a man all Kansans can be proud of. The house where Dwight Eisenhower lived as a boy is now part of the Eisenhower Center in Abilene. Be sure you visit this wonderful museum.

Chapter Twenty:
Rails West!

"By the time Kansas Territory was formed in 1854, however, people were talking about the wonder of the age—the railroad."

"Do you remember how the first pioneers traveled to Kansas? Many came in wagons and stagecoaches. Others came on the steamboats which chugged up the Missouri River."

A locomotive of the Kansas Pacific Railroad.

"Iron horses" at the railroad roundhouse.

Iron rails had been laid in many states in the East, and steam engines were successfully pulling cars over these rails.

It was hard to believe the stories that were told about the "iron horse." The trains traveled at speeds up to fifteen miles an hour! Imagine that! And they didn't get stuck in the mud! And in one day a train covered the distance it took a covered wagon two weeks to go. Unbelievable!

The pioneer town-builders in Kansas were, of course, anxious to have railroads built to their new towns. Dozens of railroad companies were formed in the 1850's but not until 1860 did a locomotive run on the tracks laid on Kansas soil. This took place at Elwood. A few miles of the tracks had been built. A locomotive and cars were ferried across the Missouri River and placed on the track. The people of Elwood went wild—a new age had come—the age of the "iron horse."

These folks were disappointed, however, for their railroad stopped operation—just about as soon as it started. Conditions were not right for railroad building.

After the Civil War, however, railroad building began in real earnest. And in a few years hundreds of miles of railroad were built.

Money to pay for the railroads came from several sources. The United States government gave money and land to several of the larger railroads. The State also gave money to support railroad construction; and counties and cities gladly raised money to give to the railroad companies.

The point is, Kansans wanted railroads, and they were willing "to pay for the whistle," as the pioneer expresssion put it. They would do anything to get the railroads built.

Here is an example. The leaders of McPherson wanted a railroad very badly. Several times the residents of the county were asked to vote money to give to a railroad company. After several unsuccessful attempts, the supporters of the railroad finally got the voters to say, "Yes". $20,000 was raised by the sale of county bonds. The money was given to a railroad which was building east from Marion County. The "iron horse" arrived in McPherson in May, 1879.

"A grand celebration was held in the city, attended by citizens of both counties to the number of 6,000 or 7,000. By eleven o'clock the streets were crowded with people, and at noon the first train arrived from Marion County bringing nearly 2,000 visitors. The multitude helped themselves from five long tables, bountifully spread, and all went happy as a marriage ball. McPherson was, in fact, married to the outside world."

The railroad depot became the center of town. And the town-builders rejoiced! They knew that their towns were bound to prosper—now that the railroad had come!

A railroad depot in Topeka.

There was one thing the town-builders had not counted on. They did not know that the railroad companies wanted to lay out and to develop their own towns!

Suppose a town-builder staked out his town on the Kansas prairie before the railroad was built. A year or two later a railroad starts to build his way. The town-builder goes to the railroad's officers and invites them to build into his town. The railroad men smile and tell him they will build to his town **if** he hands over to them most of the town site and a sum of money.

What can the town-builder do? For one thing, he can do what the folks of Ladore did. They refused to meet the railroad's demand and they watched the tracks laid around their town—and the railroad lay out the town of Parsons. They knew they were defeated; they put their buildings on rollers and moved them into Parsons.

The same thing happened to "Buffalo Bill" Cody. He and a friend laid out the town of Rome in Ellis County. Rome grew rapidly. It soon had about two hundred buildings. But the railroad built its own town a few miles east of Rome. Cody's town went out of business, and Buffalo Bill moved to Hays City, the railroad's town, to live. In fact, Bill went to work for the railroad. He was paid $500 a month to bring in twelve buffalo a day to provide meat for the construction crews. This is how Bill became known as "Buffalo Bill".

This monument stands at the site of Rome, the town "Buffalo Bill" Cody unsuccessfully promoted.

The railroad companies, of course, wanted people to come to Kansas. The more people who lived in the towns and on the land, the more business there would be for the railroads.

The Federal government gave land to several railroads. The idea was for the railroads to sell the land and to use the money to pay for building their lines.

The railroads offered these lands for sale, usually at reasonable prices. They advertised the lands and did everything they could to persuade people to come to Kansas.

Mile by mile the railroads crept across the Kansas prairie. The railroad hired settlers to build the roads. Money earned by laying track was then used by the pioneer farmers and ranchers to buy the land, stock and equipment they needed to get started.

The Kansas Pacific, or the Union Pacific, was built from the Missouri River to Denver. It was one of the main lines in Kansas. Tracks were laid during good weather. Construction stopped in the winter, and a temporary town sprang up at the end of the track.

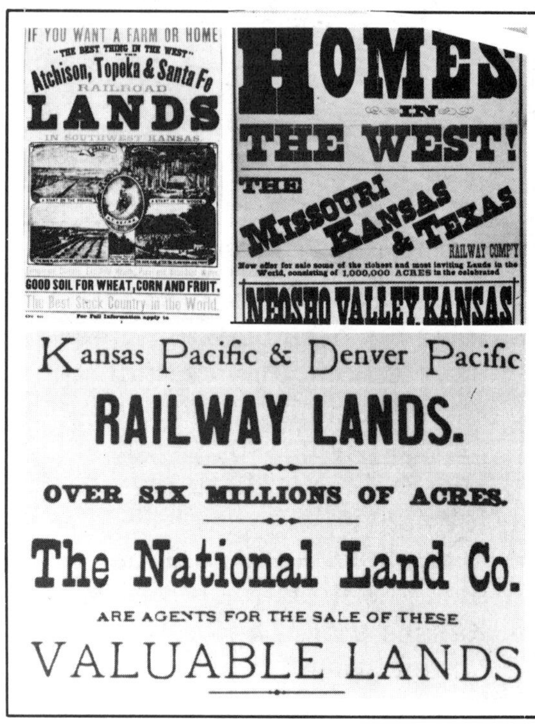

These "end-of-track" towns were wild places. In 1869 end-of-track was in Logan County and the town of

Sheridan sprang up.

A reporter for a eastern newspaper visited Sheridan. He saw that the railroad ran down the middle of the main street. On either side of this one street were stores, a few hotels and about fifty saloons and gambling houses which operated night and day.

As the train approached the town, the engineer slowed down so his passengers could see if any bodies were hanging from the trestle outside of town.

The next year "end-of-track" moved into Colorado. Sheridan disappeared.

Railroad pioneers in western Kansas.

The railroad builders faced many problems in western Kansas. They put up with heat, dust and shortages of water and food. But a major problem was hostile Indians.

The Indians hated the railroads. They knew that the trains brought hunters who wiped out the herds of buffalo. And they knew also that the "iron horse" brought in settlers to occupy the land.

The angry Indians tore up the railroad tracks.

They attacked construction crews. Railroad workers killed by Indians are buried in Victoria and Russell.

Soldiers from posts in western Kansas tried to protect the railroad workers, but they had a real job on their hands.

These men, stationed a Fort Wallace, attempted to keep the hostile Indians under control.

The railroad pioneers overcame all obstacles. The railroads were built, and Kansas grew and prospered as a result of the coming of the "iron horse."

Fort Hays was built to provide protection for the railroad.

Fort Hays

The railroad pioneers would be amazed to see the modern locomotives which roar across Kansas.

PICTURE POWER!

This kind of thing happened frequently in western Kansas in the early days of railroading.

1. What is happening in the picture?
2. If you were riding on the train, what would you be doing right now?
3. Were the buffalo afraid of the trains? How can you tell?
4. What would be the best way to get the buffalo off the track?

Chapter Twenty-One:
Sod-Busters

Perhaps some of your ancestors were pioneer Kansas farmers. Thousands of pioneers came to Kansas just for that reason. They wanted to own their own farms.

Settlers coming into Greenwood County.

A Pioneer Family Comes to Kansas

The story of Olive Clark and her family begins in Iowa.

"In October, 1867, father became infected with that contagious disease known as 'Kansas Fever'. Early in the month of November he sold the farm... for twelve hundred dollars and bought an outfit for immigration to Kansas with Osage county the objective.

Our outfit consisted of two covered wagons containing eatables, our personal effects and some few household necessities. These wagons behind which were led two milch cows for the purpose of furnishing milk for the family, were drawn by four head of horses or one team to each wagon. This, I think, was the sum of our possessions at the beginning of our trip from Iowa to Kansas.

[Apparently Olive's father changed his mind about going to Osage County, for he led his family to Ottawa County in north central Kansas. Near Minneapolis he made a deal with a settler. The settler traded his claim to Olive's father for a horse.]

Mother did not agree with this plan and she, being an outspoken woman, made the remark that she'd be darned if she'd hole up like a prairie dog, and that she didn't see why a man of good sound judgment would want to bring his family to such a God-forsaken country anyway, but of course, Mother, like all pioneer women of those days, sacrificed her ideals and consented to father's plans.

The men and women who came to Kansas obtained land in several ways.

They could buy land from the railroads. They could also buy land from the United States government.

The State of Kansas also had land for sale.

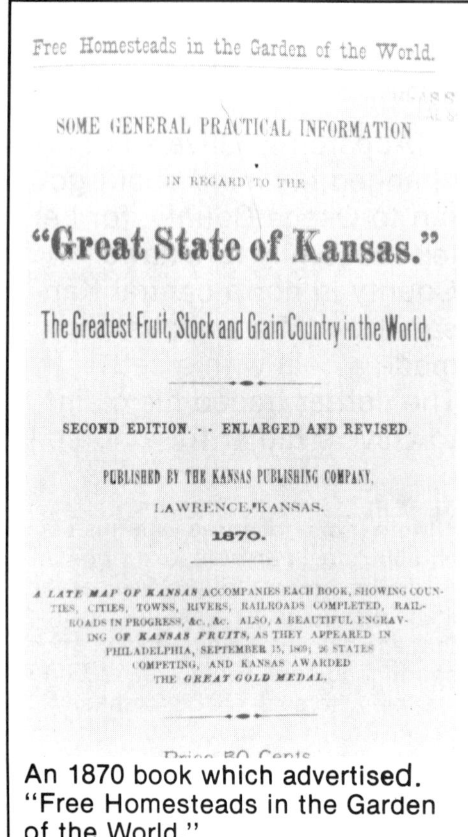

Free Homesteads in the Garden of the World.

SOME GENERAL PRACTICAL INFORMATION

IN REGARD TO THE

"Great State of Kansas."

The Greatest Fruit, Stock and Grain Country in the World.

SECOND EDITION. - - ENLARGED AND REVISED.

PUBLISHED BY THE KANSAS PUBLISHING COMPANY,

LAWRENCE, KANSAS.

1870.

A LATE MAP OF KANSAS ACCOMPANIES EACH BOOK, SHOWING COUNTIES, CITIES, TOWNS, RIVERS, RAILROADS COMPLETED, RAILROADS IN PROGRESS, &c., &c. ALSO, A BEAUTIFUL ENGRAVING OF *KANSAS FRUITS*, AS THEY APPEARED IN PHILADELPHIA, SEPTEMBER 15, 1869; 26 STATES COMPETING, AND KANSAS AWARDED THE *GREAT GOLD MEDAL*.

An 1870 book which advertised. "Free Homesteads in the Garden of the World."

After 1863 settlers could get free land from the United States government. The Homestead law said that any man or woman could have 160 acres of land, free, if they would live on the land for five years.

Ten years later Congress passed another law. This law said that a settler could have another 160 acres of land free, if he or she would plant trees on part of the claim. Perhaps one of your pioneer ancestors received a "tree claim" under this law.

The important point to remember is this: pioneer farmers obtained their land in different ways. Not all of them homesteaded on free land. Many of them bought their land.

A western Kansas land office.

What kind of land did the pioneers want?

Those who settled in eastern Kansas wanted land along streams and rivers. They could get water from the streams; but, more important, trees grew along the streams. The trees would furnish building material, fencing and fuel for the settlers.

Moreover, in these days people believed that crops would grow only in the valleys. The prairie land, away from the river valleys, was considered to be infertile —unfit for raising crops.

Many settlers had a hard time finding land. But once they found a piece of land they went to the local land office to register their claims.

A land office in Sedgwick County, 1873.

Even after making the trip to the land office and registering the claim, a settler was still not sure he would hang on to his land. Claim-jumpers were always around, ready to seize a piece of land if they could.

This interesting plaque hangs in the Sherman County Courthouse in Goodland. The letters H.U.A. stand for the Homesteaders' Union Association. When this county was being settled, the pioneers had trouble with claim-jumpers. The H.U.A. was formed to fight the claim-jumpers, and it did a good job helping settlers hold their land.

After moving to their land, the pioneers started at once to build their houses.

In eastern Kansas houses were made of logs.

This pioneer log cabin stands in the park in Ottawa. It was built by Jacob Dietrich in 1859.

Where there were no trees to cut down and use to build log cabins, the pioneers had to build other kinds of houses.

Some settlers lived in dugouts like this one in Dickinson County. A hole was dug in the ground and covered with a roof—not all dugouts had a good board roof like this one.

A stovepipe in the roof carried away the smoke from the stove. A wooden door kept out the wind and rain.

One family of very poor pioneers lived in a dugout. They slept on the floor. The father remembered seeing the members of the family "make up their beds with a hoe!" I think he was just joking.

In western Kansas the pioneers built sod houses. To build a soddie, the pioneer first plowed up long strips of sod. Then he cut the strips into pieces about two feet long. These pieces were then laid one on top of another, making the walls of the house.

This man is cutting sod which will be used to make a sod house.

It didn't take long to make a sod house, and the house didn't cost much to build, either. L.L. Scott homesteaded in Ness County. He built a sod house that measured sixteen by eighteen feet. It cost him $7.00. Three dollars were used to purchase lumber for a door and several windows. Four dollars went to buy a "large elm tree . . . the first 8 ft. was used for a center post in the middle of the room; the next 20 ft. went into the ridge pole." He then used large branches to finish off the roof, and he covered the roof with two layers of sod, grass side down.

The Metcalfe sod house in Decatur County.

A well-built sod house made a snug home. Since the walls were about two feet thick, the house was cool in the summer and warm in the winter.

The roof was the only real problem. Sod and branch roofs, like the one Mr. Scott made, usually leaked badly. And in dry weather dirt constantly dropped form the roof. Children would be awakened at night by pieces of sod falling in their faces.

Pioneer mothers tried to make the houses comfortable. They fought a never-ending battle with the dirt. And they pasted newspapers on the walls. Newspapers used in this way were known as "homesteaders' wallpaper."

There was one problem with this kind of wallpaper. One Kansas mother remembered that her children would stand around and "read the walls" rather than doing their chores. One mother fooled her family. She put the newspaper on the walls upside down. Then the children no longer stood around and "read the walls."

No matter how hard they worked, or what they did, pioneer mothers could not rid the soddie of bugs and fleas.

They scrubbed the floor and walls with kerosene. They covered the walls with newspaper. But nothing worked. The bugs and fleas always returned to keep the family company.

During warm weather the family made up their beds outside the house on the ground or in a haystack. They just let the bugs and fleas have the house to themselves!

Rattlesnakes and bullsnakes were frequent visitors in the sod houses. Once in a while a snake would fall from the roof—right into the middle of the table where the family was eating.

There are many pioneer stories about snakes crawling into the babies' beds to keep warm. You can bet that pioneer mothers always had a strong stick or a hoe at hand with which to kill the hated snakes.

A Finney County soddie.

Once the house was finished and the family moved in, the pioneer father tried to find a water supply.

In western Kansas one homesteader went three miles to a stream to get water for his family. One day a neighbor asked him why he didn't dig a well so he wouldn't have to carry water three miles. The man replied, "It's three miles down to water. I just as soon walk as dig a well that deep!"

This fellow was exaggerating, to be sure. But in central and western Kansas pioneers did have to dig deep wells to obtain water.

And well-digging was very difficult and dangerous. Men would start digging a well—as they went deeper and deeper, the danger of the walls caving in on them increased. And there was always the danger of men suffocating at the bottom of the deep wells.

So, for the Kansas pioneers it was a wonderful victory when they had their very own well—and a windmill whirring in the breeze —bringing them the water they needed.

A Kansas pioneer gathers cowchips.

The family now had a house and a supply of water. What next? They needed a supply of fuel for their stoves.

Trees were soon cut down and used for fuel. Then the pioneers had to drive long miles to find a wagon load of firewood.

Coal was available in eastern Kansas. But many homesteaders and settlers could not affort to buy coal.

So they burned whatever they could find—hay, weeds, corn stalks—but especially, prairie coal. What is "prairie coal"? Cow-chips, that's what. By using cow-chips the pioneers solved their energy shortage.

Most of the time pioneer families had enough to eat. Every meal, however, consisted of the same food. Many of their dishes were made from corn. They also ate home-baked bread and salted or dried meat.

In summer, of course, they would have vegetables from the garden. This was a welcome change. And the men would bring in game they had killed on the prairie. One Kansas pioneer said he killed 600 prairie chickens in one month!

The children had fun gathering wild fruit and berries.

What happened when someone had an accident or

became ill? Most of the time doctors could not be called—the towns, where the doctors lived, were too far away.

Luckily, however, there were people like Amy Loucks in every pioneer community.

Mrs. Loucks was born in Pennsylvania and came to Kearny County in 1879. Her brother was a doctor, and Mrs. Loucks had learned something about medicine from him. So, she was of real help and comfort to her Kansas neighbors.

On one occasion a man was brought to her house who had been scalped by the Indians and left on the prairie. She stitched up his wounds with a fiddle string and a needle and nursed him back to health. Another time a man was brought to her with a severe bullet wound. Using a knitting needle, she removed the bullet and saved the man's life.

A railroad worker crushed his hand; she used a razor to amputate three fingers. She was called to the railroad depot to meet a train and help a woman deliver her baby. And when a railroad wreck occurred near her home, she administered first aid to the injured.

Mrs. Loucks was a real pioneer heroine! But most pioneer mothers did the same things she did.

Mothers usually had some home-made medicines on hand. A mixture of onion juice and turpentine, for example, was used as a cough medicine.

The pioneers seemed to have one rule about medicines: the worse the medicine tasted, the better it was for you!

Ague was a disease which afflicted most pioneer families. It was a form of fever, or malaria, which just hung on and on. Abbie Bright and her brother homesteaded in Sedgwick County, and they, and their neighbors all suffered with ague. Abbie wrote the following in her diary:

"So many have, or had the ague, I believe it is always so in new settlements. Brother is getting well slowly, but his appetite is poor. Had intended having soup for dinner of the buffalo

meat, but was too inexperienced to make it for company. We had (it) for supper, however, and it was good, and he ate a little of it. It is terrible to be sick, out on the frontier."

Some problems, however, just could not be avoided. The Woody family lived in a dugout in Ottawa County. Mr. and Mrs. Woody and their baby went to bed one night, all in the same bed. Suddenly, a huge cow came falling through the roof. The local newspaper reported, "Mr. Woody finally got the steer off the bed and looked after the injuries of his wife and child. This is a great country, where cattle wander on top of the houses and fall in on people while they are asleep."

And what about the Kansas weather?

Andrew Rinhart came to Garden City from Indiana. He was a carpenter. He said he appreciated the Kansas wind—he just put a board up on the side of a house, let the wind hold it in place while he drove in the nails. Great country!

It did get warm in Kansas, once in a while. It was said that farmers could not raise popcorn in Kansas. One fellow tried and the heat caused the popcorn to pop out of the cob and cover the ground. The man went out to inspect the field, saw that his field was completely white, thought it was snow and promptly froze to death.

Remember that many folks said that Kansas was a desert country where it never rained?

There were years of drought, when it did not rain enough to raise crops. But at other times, there was more rain than the settlers wanted. And sometimes a storm brought a tragedy, as it did in Nemaha County.

One Sunday in March, 1897, Mrs. McGrath hitched up the wagon, loaded in her six children and started to the neighbors for a visit. They came to a creek. The water was high because of recent rains. The mother hesitated. She didn't think she should try to cross the swollen stream. But the children begged and coaxed. They were looking forward to their visit with the neighbor's children.

Mother McGrath drove the team into the stream. The horses tried to turn around in the high water. The wagon overturned, and Mrs. McGrath and the children were swept away. Mrs. McGrath managed to pull herself from the icy stream—all the children drowned. A terrible pioneer tragedy.

Then there were the Kansas blizzards. One of the worst storms in Kansas history howled over the plains on Easter weekend, 1873.

A week or so before the great blizzard, the Crane family, who lived in Republic County, had their house destroyed by a prairie fire. Mrs. Crane and her three children moved in with their neighbors, the Bennetts.

The storm started on Easter Sunday. The wind ripped the roof from the house where the two families huddled. Mr. Bennett went for help, and when he returned he found his wife and four children and Mrs. Crane and two of her children—frozen to death.

This stone marks the grave of Mrs. Bennett and her four children who perished in the Easter blizzard of 1873.

Did you notice in the story of the Crane family and the Easter blizzard that their house had been destroyed in a prairie fire?

Prairie fires were another problem faced by the prairie pioneers. In the fall of the year the dry prairie grass caught fire easily.

Settlers plowed "fire guards" around their houses and barns. Town-builders hired men to plow "guards" around their towns.

Prairie fires were a real danger to a wooden town, such as Concordia.

Every person turned out to fight the dreaded prairie fires.

But every year prairie fires roared over the Kansas prairies. Houses, barns and haystacks went up in smoke. Even worse, people were trapped in the flames and burned to death. In Nicodemus, Black pioneer mothers wrapped their children in wet blankets and put them in holes in the ground to protect them from prairie fires.

Parents warned their children to watch for prairie fires. If the children saw clouds of smoke rising on the horizon, they were to run for home—fast!

During the summers of 1874 and 1875 the prairie pioneers faced another terrible problem—grasshoppers!

This is how the grasshoppers came.

A family of pioneers is sitting around the dinner table in their sod house. Suddenly, they notice that it has become very dark.

"Must be a storm coming up," says Father.

The family leaves the table and walks outside for a look. But the clouds in the northwest do not look like the usual storm clouds.

"Pa, what kid of clouds are those?" asks Mother.

Before he can answer, grasshoppers start to fall from the sky—billions and billions of the insects. They begin to devour every green plant in sight.

Father yells, "Hurry, everybody! Get your brooms and rakes! I'll start a fire, and we'll try to burn up these terrible grasshoppers!"

But it was useless to try to burn up the 'hoppers. There were just too many of them.

In Brown County railroad trains couldn't run on the tracks. The masses of 'hoppers, crushed beneath the wheels of the locomotive, made the tracks too slippery for traction.

A train stopped by grasshoppers

One pioneer farmer in northeastern Kansas said that his land looked as though a tornado had crossed it. Every stalk of corn and wheat—every tree—had been stripped by the insects.

Read the account written by a pioneer of Rice County —a "voice from the past."

"For the first three days after the appearance of the grasshoppers, the whole heavens were darkened with their presence and the earth with their bodies. They covered every tree and plant and every green thing—the prairie and water courses. They flew like hail in the faces of men, dashed themselves against every object...and as they rushed through the air or near the earth and struck an opposing object, the rattle of their contact resembled the sound of a hailstorm on the roof, or the clashing of sabres in the scabbards of a squadron of cavalry at full gallop..."

A settler in Allen County remembered that the grasshoppers piled up in the fields—the 'hoppers looked like drifts of snow covering the fields.

After the grasshoppers devastated the land, many settlers gave up and left Kansas. But there were pioneers who refused to give up. Back in the East people collected food, clothing and money and sent these relief supplies to the people of Kansas.

E.D. Haney lived in Cloud County, and he remembered that a box of clothing arrived from Massachusetts. In the big box, he said, was an amazing assortment of "stuff"—men's top hats; ladies' ball gowns; dancing shoes. But the settlers made use of every article of clothing. And that which they could not use they sold, and the money was used to buy food for the settlers who were in need.

Yes, the prairie pioneers faced many hardships. Back in pioneer days the girls used water in buckets for mirrors—no one owned a glass mirror. A pioneer wife said that during the first year of her marriage, she and her husband spent $16.00 in cash—that is all the money they had for the entire year.

But the pioneers also had good times! Henry Horst, who had a claim in Logan County, said that the settlers always found time to have fun. They had many pleasant times at the school house.

Mr. Horst, a "voice from the past":

"I do not wish to leave the impression that only hard times existed in Western Kansas, and that we had no time for recreation. The little white school houses dotted the prairies in every direction, and those were the gathering

Dugout school in Thomas County.

places for young and old. Many a happy hour have we spent in these places of eduction, where community entertainments, Fourth of July celebrations, Christmas doings, and many other happy events were held and enjoyed by all. Besides these affairs in the country, the town of Oakley provided much recreation in the shape of races, fairs, and other entertainments which drew large crowds..."

Elam Bartholomew homesteaded in Rooks County in the 1870's. He kept a diary of his family's activities. And they did many, many things together. They went to town, usually two or three times a week, just to visit. They attended literary society meetings and "singing schools" at the school house. There were Christmas parties and box socials to enjoy.

And the Bartholomews were never lonesome. In 1880 more than a thousand persons—that's right, a thousand persons—visited in their home. And Mrs. Bartholomew served meals to 738 persons over three years of age! Mrs. Bartholomew might have become very weary—but she was certainly never lonesome!

Osborn, Kansas, Farmer, 1877

We are living in a fast age. We have fast women, fast men and fast farmers. . . . We have all the modern improvements it seems necessary to have to do fast work; but brains are needed to make farming a success in such an age as ours.

At the Post Rock Museum in La Crosse, you will discover the story of the prairie pioneers.

Chapter Twenty-Two
Cowpunchers and Longhorns

As you know, huge herds of buffalo once roamed the hills, valleys and prairies of Kansas.

You also know that the plains Indians hunted the buffalo for food. Just about everything the Indians needed for food and clothing came from the buffalo.

A buffalo hunter's camp in Kansas.

The covered wagon pioneers were always excited when they saw their first buffalo. The men in the wagon trains shot many buffalo, but there were still thousands and thousands of buffalo left for the Indians.

Then the railroads came into buffalo country. The trains brought white hunters with high-powered rifles. These hunters began to kill the buffalo by the thousands.

The hunters were interested in taking the hides from the dead buffalo. The hides were then taken to towns like Dodge City and shipped back east to be made into leather.

A pile of buffalo hides awaits shipment at Dodge City.

With the white hunters engaged in their deadly work, the buffalo herds grew smaller and smaller. The Indians became very angry. They hated the buffalo hunters who slaughtered the buffalo.

The killing of the buffalo, more than any other thing, caused the Indians of western Kansas to go on the warpath. They fought to keep the white hunters from killing the buffalo; and they fought to keep white settlers from taking over their hunting grounds.

The monument tells the story of the peace treaty signed between the Indians and the whites at Medicine Lodge.

From time to time the government tried to make peace with the Indians. In 1867 leaders of the Kiowa, Apache, Comanche, Arapaho and Cheyenne Indians came to Medicine Lodge. The Indians promised to stop fighting and to accept the help of the government in becoming peaceful farmers.

The conference at Medicine Lodge. Drawn by a man who was present at the conference.

But the treaties between the Indians and the whites were never honored. Both sides broke the agreements, and war would again sweep the prairie.

In the cemetery of old Fort Wallace is a marker that tells the tragic story of the German family.

In the late summer of 1874 the German family—father, mother and seven children—were crossing western Kansas in a covered wagon. Mr. German was foolish. It was a mistake to travel Indian country in this way.

Somewhere along the stage road in Logan County, Indians attacked the German family. The Indians killed Mr. and Mrs. German and three of their children. Four girls were taken into captivity: Catherine, aged 17; Sophia, 12; Julia, 7 and Addie, 5.

The two little girls were frightened and cried constantly. The Indians dumped them on the prairie and left them. For six weeks these two little girls lived on the prairie, eating berries and

Addie and Julia German, shortly after their rescue.

plant roots. They were finally rescued.

The war between the whites and the Indians went on for many years. Finally the Indians surrendered. Many of the Indians were sent to reservations in what is now the State of Oklahoma. Among the Indians sent to Oklahoma were the Northern Cheyennes, who had lived in Montana and Wyoming before the war began.

The Cheyenne hated their reservation, and in 1878 a group of the Indians decided to escape from the reservation and return to their homeland in Wyoming and Montana.

As the Indians, under their chief Dull Knife, crossed Kansas, heading north, they were pursued by soldiers.

In this rock-filled canyon in Scott County, the soldiers attacked the Cheyenne.

The Indian men hid their women and children in this cave. They then fought off the soldiers and made good their escape.

In Decatur County the Indians raided settlers' homes. They killed settlers and stole horses. Finally, these Indians were captured by soldiers in Nebraska. The homesick Cheyenne failed in their effort to return to their homes. This was the last Indian fighting in Kansas.

In the Oberlin Cemetery are the graves of some of the settlers killed by the Cheyenne Indians in 1878.

Now we must look at what was happening in Texas, far to the south of Kansas.

In Texas there were ranchers who owned thousands of longhorn cattle. But the ranchers could not find a market for their cattle.

Then the railroads began to build west across Kansas. The cattlemen had an idea. They would drive their cattle north to these railroads. Men who wanted to buy the longhorns would meet the Texas cattlemen at towns along the railroads.

There were northern cattlemen who also thought this was a good idea. One of them was Joseph G. McCoy of Illinois. He selected the little railroad town of Abilene as his market town. And he sent word to the Texans: Drive your cattle to Abilene and there will be men waiting there to buy your herds!

So the Texas cattlemen formed their herds. A herd usually consisted of from two to three thousand longhorns.

And they hired men to drive the herd north to Kansas. Most of these trail hands were young fellows. Some of them were no more than fifteen years old.

An experienced cowboy would be made the trail boss. He would be in charge of a crew of ten to twelve men. One man, known as the wrangler, spent all his time caring for the horses. And this was a big job, for each cowboy had five or six horses.

Trail hands at chuck wagon meal.

The trail boss and the hands rode with the herd all day. The cowboys with the least experience rode behind the herd, making sure that none of the "drags" wandered away from the herd. This was the worst job a trail hand could have. They "ate dirt" all day.

Late in the day the cattle were stopped and the cowboys let them settle down for the night.

All through the night the cowboys took turns riding around the herd. Usually they sang softly; the music helped quiet the animals.

The trail hands soon learned to get along without much sleep. The boss told them they could catch up on their sleep once they got the herd delivered to the Kansas cowtown.

A very important member of the trail crew was the cook. In his chuck wagon the cook carried all the things he needed to prepare meals for the men. One thing for sure: the cowboys never argued with the cook. The cook was the "king" of the camp.

The trip from Texas to the Kansas cowtowns might take as long as three months. The longhorns would cover twenty miles on a good day—but there were always delays.

In dry weather the thirsty cattle refused to move along the trail. The herd would have to be driven far from the trail in order to find a water hole.

Then, the cattle might stampede. Stampedes came at any time, night or day. One minute the longhorns would be behaving just fine. Next minute the whole herd would be off and running.

After a bad stampede it might take the hands several days to get all the critters rounded up.

The herds also lost time at the river crossings. The rivers were usually running high and deep in the spring. The cowboys drove the cattle into the river and then rode after them.

Crossing the rivers was the most difficult, and most dangerous, part of the trail drive.

After long days on the trail, the herd of longhorns and the exhausted trail-hands came to the end of the trail. Ahead lay a Kansas cowtown on the railroad.

The trail boss rode ahead and met with the cattle buyers. A deal for the cattle was made. The cattle were drive to the "pens" along the tracks. The buyer handed over the money, and the trail boss returned to camp and paid off the trail hands.

The boys were really happy now. With coins jingling in their pockets, they took off for town.

A cowtown dance hall.

Most of the trail hands went first to the stores and bought the supplies they needed for the coming year.

But there were always some of the boys who didn't have good sense. They went right to the saloons and gambling houses. In a few hours all their hard-earned money was gone.

Loading Texas longhorns in Abilene.

Dodge City. A Kansas cattle town.

Kansas had many famous cattle towns—Abilene, Ellsworth, Caldwell, Wichita, Newton and Dodge City.

Everyone knows that these cattle towns were wide-open places. They certainly were that, but in most of the towns efforts were made to maintain law and order.

On this corner "Wild Bill" shot down a gambler—and by accident killed one of his deputies.

In Abilene, for example, a number of famous lawmen walked the streets. Among them was the famous "Wild Bill" Hickok.

But men like "Wild Bill" have gotten more publcity than they deserve. In Abilene, for example, the lawman who did an outstanding job was Tom Smith. But Tom is practically unknown—he didn't get the publicity that "Wild Bill" had showered upon him.

Tom Smith, Abilene lawman.

In the cemetery in Hays there is the grave of Sheriff Alexander Ramsey, who was killed by outlaws June 5, 1875. The marker tells another side of the story of law and order on the frontier —notice that his wife is buried here too. She died eleven days after her husband was killed. It is said she died of a broken heart.

Using the Texas cattle and the land which was now cleared of Indians and buffalo, Kansas cattlemen began to establish ranches. Men who had worked as trailhands now signed on to work for the ranchers.

The cowboys were interesting fellows. Most of them were young men. As a rule they didn't talk much about themselves. But most of them probably grew up on farms. Some came from Eastern cities, and it was not unusual for a cowboy to show, by his speech and manners, that he was educated.

You could always tell a cowboy by his clothing. He wore a tall, broad-brimmed hat that kept the sun from burning his face and neck. The hat also could be used to carry water for his horse.

A handkerchief around the neck could be pulled up to cover his nose and mouth. The handkerchief kept the dust from choking him.

High-heeled boots kept his foot in the stirrup. The heel was shaped in such a way, however, that it would slip easily out of the stirrup in case the cowboy fell out of the saddle.

One thing every cowboy feared—being "hung up." That is, have a foot caught in the stirrup after he had fallen from the saddle—and being dragged by the runaway horse.

And don't think that cowboys never were thrown. As an old cowboy once said, "There never was a horse that couldn't be rode, and a cowboy that couldn't be throwed!"

Of course, you seldom saw the cowboy without his horse. Cowboys wore tight, high-heeled boots just so they would have an excuse not to walk. There is the story of one Kansas rancher who always kept a saddled horse outside his house. When he had to go to the barn, which was just a few hundred feet away from the house, he rode the horse.

A fellow asked him why he rode the horse instead of walking. The rancher said, "If God had intended men to walk, He would have given them four feet!"

The cowboys took good care of their horses. Only in an emergency would a man gallop his horse. I'm sure old-time cowboys are really mad when they watch TV cowboys gallop their horses all the time. No real cowboy would wear out a good horse that way.

The same thing is true of six-guns. Old time cowboys seldom wore guns when they worked. They just got in the way. A few would strap on their pistols when they went into town, but then the guns were more for show than anything else.

What about spurs? On many Kansas ranches cowboys were not permitted to wear spurs. One rancher said that good cowboys did not need spurs. Only those men who weren't good at handling horses had to wear spurs.

For a few years the cattle ranchers made good money. But then cattle prices began to drop, and in the late 1880's terrible storms swept the prairie. Cattle by the thousands died, and many ranchers went out of business.

Before the cattlemen could recover from these hard times, farmers began to take over the range country.

For years cowboys spread the story that it never rained west of Dodge City. No one, they claimed, would ever be able to farm in that dry country.

But in the 1880's folks began to believe that the climate in western Kansas was changing. Rainfall was increasing! The increase in rainfall resulted from the fact that farmers were breaking the sod. This permitted moisture to escape into the air—and so increase the rainfall.

"Rainfall follows the plow!" That's what they believed, and thousands of families moved into western Kansas, to plow the prairie and to make their farms.

For a few years everything went fine. Then it stopped raining. Crops burned up. Farmers went broke, and many left the land.

Those who remained decided they would go into cattle ranching, and their descendants are still on the ranches, raising fine Kansas cattle.

Some of the Texas cowboys went to work for Kansas ranchers. They soon learned that "punching" cattle was not easy. The cowpunchers worked long hours and didn't get very good pay.

But these cowpunchers were important Kansas pioneers. In many parts of Kansas, as you "listen to the land," you'll hear the story of the cowpunchers and the longhorns.

It is hard to believe, but this street in Wichita was once a cattle trail.

A Story of the Texas Trail

One day a young boy walked into a cow camp in Texas. He begged the trail boss to give him a job.

"You look very young," said the boss. "We're driving these cattle all the way to Kansas. You sure you can do the work?"

"You bet I can, sir," replied the boy. "Just give me a chance."

So the boss hired "The Kid," as he became known to the other cowpunchers. He turned out to be a good worker. He would take any job without complaining. He didn't swear and he didn't chew tobacco. The other cowhands liked him.

The herd moved slowly north. The cattle walked into Kansas. One night while they were camped near a small Kansas town, the Kid came up to the boss and said, "Boss, I'm homesick. I want my pay so I can go home."

The trail boss understood. So he gave the Kid his hard-earned money, shook his hand and wished him luck. The Kid turned and headed toward town.

A few hours later a young lady, all dressed up in a new gown, walked into the camp. The boss looked at the girl—then cried out, "My gosh, the Kid's a girl!"

Yes, it turned out that the Kid was the daughter of a rancher from Caldwell, Kansas. She wanted to ride the Texas trail, like the young men did. And she showed these Texas cowboys that she could do the job.

"Why don't you go to your People Bank. Find the names of men and women who have lived on ranches. Invite them to tell the story of their ranches to your class."

"And there may be some of you students who live on ranches today. Why don't you discover the story of your ranch and share that story with the class? They would enjoy hearing the story of the ranch where you live."

Chapter Twenty-Three
From Many Lands

Let's talk about the prairie pioneers who came to Kansas from foreign lands. Your ancestors were among these pioneers, so you need to know about them.

Why did these people decide to make the long, hard trip to Kansas?

One reason was because Kansas, in the United States, meant opportunity and freedom.

In Kansas these immigrants could get land. They could open businesses. Their children would go to school. And they would be free to attend whatever church they desired.

In the old countries, the countries across the sea, your ancestors did not have these opportunities and freedoms.

Yes, that is true. People in Europe and in other parts of the world were not free. Poor people had no chance of ever owning land. They paid high taxes to support the rich ruling classes. Young people were unable to find good jobs. Many did not have the right to vote. Worst of all, there were many wars fought in these lands, and young men had to serve in the army.

"So, you see, your ancestors who lived in foreign lands had many reasons for coming to Kansas."

"Here is a very important question. How did your ancestors who lived in foreign lands find out about Kansas?"

Probably the most common way they heard about Kansas was in letters they received from friends and relatives who had moved to America.

Here is the kind of letter which probably crossed the ocean to the people who still lived in the old country.

Sumner County, Kansas
United States of America
June 15, 1877

Dear Franz,

How are things in the old village? I think of you often and wish you and your family were here with us.

I have just bought my own farm. Franz, just think of it! I have a farm of 160 acres—and it is my very own.

Will you ever own your own land? Of course not. Franz, dear friend, why don't you join us in Kansas?

I will lend you money to buy your steamship ticket. Don't worry about paying me back. In just a few years you will have the money to pay what you owe me.

I know of some good land that is available. I could help you build your house and plow the land.

Come to Kansas, Franz, where you and your children will have a future!

Your friend,
Josef

Letters like this helped to convince many of our ancestors to leave the old country and come to America.

Many newspapers in Kansas were printed in foreign languages. They carried articles about this new land and urged people to come to Kansas. These newspapers were sent all over the world; and after reading about Kansas there were undoubtedly many persons who decided to come to this land of opportunity.

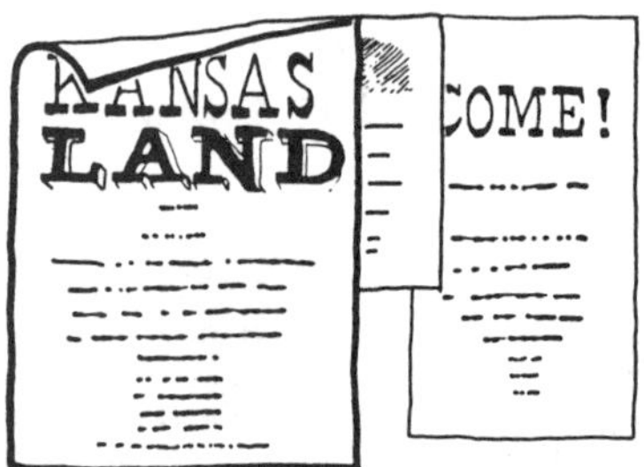

The railroad companies were especially anxious to persuade people from foreign lands to come to Kansas. The railroads had a great deal of land for sale, and they wanted people to buy the land and to open up farms and to build towns.

In particular the railroads tried to attract large groups of immigrants. It was not unusual for an entire village of people to decide to leave Europe; and the railroad companies were delighted at the chance of attracting these people to Kansas.

The railroads hired men to go to Europe and talk to the people there. These men, who were known as colonization agents, were usually natives of the land they were sent to visit. So they knew the language and they knew the people.

C.B. Schmidt was a very successful colonization agent. He was born in Germany. After arriving in Kansas he went to work for the Santa Fe Railroad. He returned to Europe as a colonization agent for that railroad, and he persuaded many people to come to Kansas.

He was particularly successful with German people who for some time had been living in Russia. These people were known as Mennonites. They were peace-loving, religious people who were excellent farmers.

The rulers of Russia decided that the Mennonite children must be taught the Russian language in the schools; and they announced that the Mennonite young men would have to serve in the Russian Army.

These people listened carefully to Mr. Schmidt's stories about Kansas. Then they sold their lands in Russia and came to America.

The women and children remained in Topeka (this photo shows them crowded together in a building in Topeka) while their menfolk and agents for the railroad looked over the land.

After arriving in America, the Mennonites climbed aboard trains for the long ride to Kansas.

At Hillsboro is a wonderful museum which tells the story of the Mennonites who settled in this part of Kansas. They lived in houses like this one—which is now the museum.

Wherever the Mennonites settled in Kansas they built fine churches. These churches were the centers of their communities.

And they farmed the land. The Mennonites brought with them wheat seed which they had used in the prairie country of Russia. This wheat was perfect for Kansas. Soon the Mennonite farmers, and other Kansas farmers, were raising huge crops of wheat and Kansas became known as the wheat State.

Pioneer monument in Victoria

Other groups of Germans left Russia, too. German Catholics settled in Ellis county. A wonderful monument, in Victoria, tells the story of the first group of twenty-three families which arrived in Ellis County in April, 1876.

The descendants of these German-Russian pioneers still live in Ellis County. Their lives still center upon the beautiful churches which their pioneer ancestors built on the Kansas prairie.

Some of our immigrant ancestors did not come directly to Kansas. They stopped for a while in eastern cities, such as Chicago and Galesburg, Illinois. The men found work in these cities, saved their money and prepared to move to Kansas.

Swedish immigrants who stopped in Chicago and Galesburg formed what were known as immigration companies. The members of the companies met and laid plans for moving to Kansas. They sent men on ahead to buy land. And when everything was arranged, the families went west, to take up their own land.

Although many of the Swedish immigrants bought farm land, not all of them were farmers. Although they were inexperienced, they worked hard. They learned how to farm. And they stayed on the land.

Coming to the new land was particularly difficult for the Swedish women. Listen to a voice from the past—Anna Berg—as she tells about her family arriving in Lindsborg, a Swedish settlement, in 1872:

"At the end of September, 1872, my mother and I arrived in Lindborg. My father had arrived some time previous and had secured an eighty acre homestead on which he had built a sod house. We were much disappointed because we had heard that everything was so wonderful in America. We had no idea of what a new settlement would be like. We were taken into the home of a neighbor, Olof Person. Mother sat down by a haystack and cried and would not go in. She wanted to return to Sweden immediately. Father comforted her by saying that they would return to Sweden as soon as money was available; with that she had to be content. We did not know that when Father came home from working on the railroad to prepare the house for our arrival he had killed six rattlers in the house..."

Sista möjligheten

att billigt erhålla

Land i Kansas.

Union Pacific R'y Co. har beslutat att bringa i marknaden återstoden af sitt land i Kansas, beläget i Thomas, St. John och Wallace counties, och som jag af jernvägsbolaget utnämts till hufvudagent för försäljningen af detta land, inbjuder jag härmed mina landsmän, att ej försumma ett tillfälle, som aldrig mer kommer att erbjudas, att skaffa sig hem, der på kort tid välmåga kan vinnas.

Jorden är af bördigaste beskaffenhet, afkastande rika skördar af hvete, råg, hafre, korn, "sorghum", "broom-corn", klöfver, frukt, bär, vindrufvor och alla slags rotfrukter; men majsen är naturligtvis hufvudskörden, alldenstund den ymniga afkastningen af detta sädesslag, på samma gång den ger uphof till en storartad kreatursafvel i allmänhet, tydligen utvisat Kansas som hufvudorten för svinafveln i Förenta Staterna.

Mesta regeringslandet är redan upptaget.

Hvad jag nu erbjuder allmänheten är derför korteligen:

Kansas-Land,

1. som aldrig förr varit i marknaden,
2. som är af aldra bästa beskaffenhet,
3. som kan fås billigt och på lång kredit,
4. som är beläget i en redan civiliserad trakt och inom området af en stat, som år 1885 hade öfver 1,270,000 invånare.

Närmare upplysningar lemnas beredvilligt genom bref eller muntligen af

Victor Rylander,

Hufvudagent U. P. R'y Co's Kansas-Land,

46 South Clark St., Chicago, Ill.

A pioneer log cabin used by Swedish pioneers near Lindsborg.

One reason the immigrant pioneers stayed on the land was because they lived among friends and neighbors. Everything was expensive. Interest rates stood at 25%! So the pioneers shared everything they had with one another.

For example, one Swedish pioneer broke his plow. He went several miles to a friend's farm and asked if he could borrow his friend's plow. "Certainly," was the reply. "Bring your oxen over, hitch them to the plow and take it home."

"I can't take the time to get the oxen," the pioneer responded. And with that, he picked up the plow, placed it over his shoulders, and carried that heavy piece of machinery home.

But these pioneers were used to hardships. Olof Erickson, a Swedish pioneer, walked forty miles to Salina to obtain some needed supplies. He walked home with his purchases on his back: a large washtub, inside of which were a sack of flour, a ham, a kerosene can, besides sacks of coffee and sugar. On top of this load was a water bucket and fifty feet of rope. And he walked forty miles with that load!

This beautiful church in Denmark, Lincoln County, stands on land settled by immigrants from Denmark.

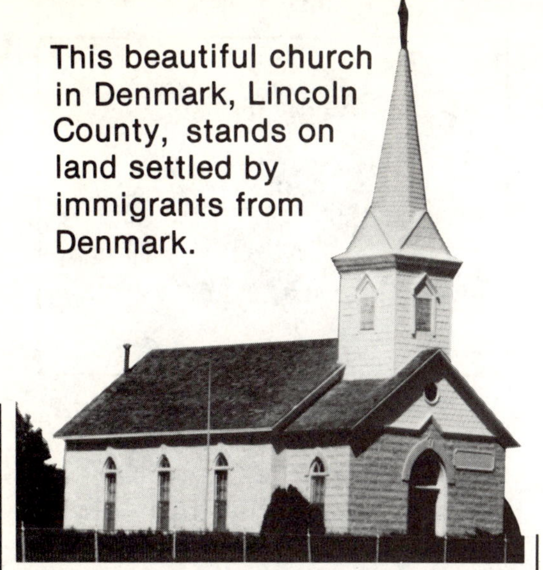

The first Danish settlers arrived in 1869—at a time when hostile Indians were prowling the land. After one bloody raid upon the settlers, a Danish boy rode to Salina with news of the Indian attack and to ask for help. He arrived in Salina and discovered that no one understood Danish—and he couldn't make the people understand what he wanted. Can you imagine how frustrated the boy must have been? Finally, however, a man who spoke Danish was found, and the boy delivered his message.

In the cemetery behind the Denmark church stands this tombstone—which tells the fascinating story of one immigrant who was born in Denmark, Europe, and who died in Denmark, Kansas.

The immigrants came from many lands. These people came from England to settle in Harper County.

This English-style mansion was erected in Sheridan County by J. Fenton Pratt. Mr. Pratt was an Englishman, and he wanted his bride, who also came

from England, to live in a house like those in England.

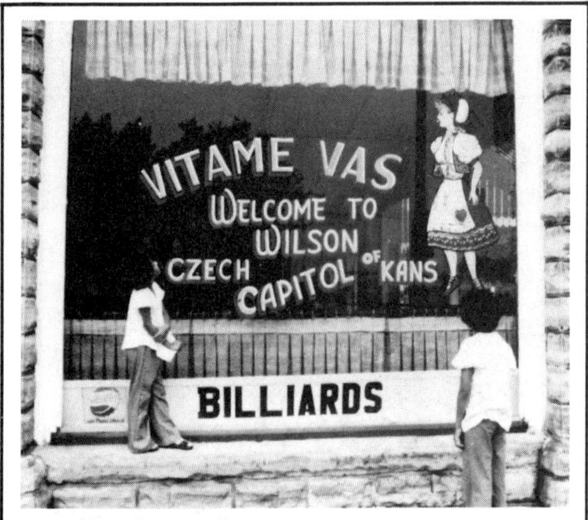

Wilson is the center of one of Kansas' Czech communities.

French immigrants took land along the Cottonwood River in eastern Kansas. Welsh pioneers lived in Lyon County. Irish immigrants took land in many parts of Kansas. Scotch Plains, a section of Republic County, was named for the Scottish people who lived there.

People from many lands came to work in the coal fields of southeastern Kansas. It is said that thirty different languages were spoken by people who lived in this part of Kansas. Imagine that!

This deserted stone schoolhouse is in Finney County. It was built in 1889.

Not far from where this school stands a group of

Jewish settlers came to build their community in 1882.

They came from Cincinatti, Ohio, and were sponsored by the Hebrew Union Agricultural Society. This organization wanted to help Jewish people get out of the crowded cities and become farmers.

The settlement was named Beersheba, for an ancient city in the Holy Land not far from Jerusalem.

The twenty-four families who came in this group had a rough time. None of them knew how to farm. The Hebrew Union Agriculture Society did not provide the aid that had been promised. And like all prairie pioneers these Jewish settlers fought dust, drought and hard times.

Finally, most of them left the land and moved into towns. Many of their descendants still live in Kansas.

Yes, the story of Kansas includes the story of these people who came from many different lands.

And it is important to remember that after these immigrants arrived in Kansas they continued to follow their foreign ways.

Those pioneers who spoke foreign languages continued to speak those languages. In many towns there were foreign-language newspapers. Church services and schools were conducted in foreign languages also. If you walked down the streets of some Kansas towns you would not hear a word of English spoken—only the foreign language of the people who lived in that town.

It was very difficult for the immigrants to give up

their language and customs. It was hard for these people to live in a strange new land, where everything was different. We can understand why they wanted to hang on to some familiar things, such as their native language.

Little by little, however, the immigrants and their children began to think of themselves as Americans. They began to give up their foreign ways of speaking and dressing.

Unfortunately there were also times when the immigrants were **forced** to give up their languages. This happened during World War I, when people who used foreign languages were considered unpatriotic and un-American. This wasn't true, of course; but the foreign pioneers were under suspicion because of their foreign ways.

In every generation people from other lands have come to Kansas. Mexican-American people came to Kansas to work on the farms and in the railroads. Today they and their children are proud to be Kansans.

And in just the last few years, people have come to Kansas from countries in southeastern Asia. Like the people of other lands who came to Kansas before them, they are also pioneers —they are preparing the way for their children and their grandchildren who will live in the free land of America.

"While all of us are proud to be citizens of the United States and of Kansas, we should also be proud of our immigrant ancestors."

"It took real courage and determination for these people to leave their native lands and come to Kansas."

"They left their homes in far away lands and came to America so that we, their descendants, might live in a free land. They came so that we might have a future."

HERITAGE SPECIAL

Black Kansans were important pioneers! Many Black families came to Kansas after the Civil War.

Some Black pioneers settled on farms, like this family in Morris County.

In Ness County a young Black man took a homestead. His name was George Washington Carver, and he became one of our nation's greatest scientists.

The marker reads: "The Carver Homestead. Citizen —Scientist—Benefactor, who rose from slavery to fame and gave to our country an everlasting heritage. Ness County is proud to honor him and claim him as a pioneer."

Black soldiers served honorably and bravely in the Indian wars.

And there were Black cowboys who rode the Kansas range.

Black Kansans share in every part of Kansas' pioneer heritage.

HERITAGE SPECIAL HERITAGE SPECIAL HERITAGE SPECIAL HERITAGE SPECIAL

UNIT SEVEN:
OUR PIONEER HERITAGE

Chapter Twenty-Four:
Kansas Today

"I know you've learned many things from Dr. Manley's book, right?"

"For one thing, you've learned that history is the story of people. You and your family are exciting parts of that story."

"Another thing—you've learned that no matter where you live in Kansas, you are surrounded by wonderful history."

"And you've learned about some important people—the pioneers of Kansas who prepared the way for you!"

The first pioneers who came to Kansas Territory lived in crude cabins.

The descendants of the pioneers built beautiful frame homes.

Today, many of you live in houses like this.

You remember that the first pioneers who came to Kansas Territory didn't know what to think about the land. Some thought that much of Kansas was desert.

But the pioneers and their children plowed the sod and harvested their crops. They proved that the land was fertile.

Oh, there were difficult times, certainly. Such as the

1930's, the "dirty 'thirties," folks called those years when the land dried up and terrible dust storms swept the plains.

But the pioneers never gave up—and neither have their descendants. Irrigation and other modern agricultural practices have made Kansas "blossom as the rose."

Just think of the kind of machinery farmers once used to work their land.

The sons of the pioneers pioneered with a new invention called the tractor.

If you don't think people's lives have changed in Kansas, just think of how your pioneer grandparents went to town.

Today, huge tractors help Kansas farmers raise the food which feeds people all over the world.

Then came the "horseless carriage," which got stuck in the creek once in a while. But it was certainly an improvement over the horse.

Today modern cars and trucks whizz over interstate highways—the ribbons of concrete laid over the old pioneer wagon trails.

Just imagine how excited your great grandpa was the day an aviator brought his flying machine to the Republic County Fair.

Little by little aviation pioneeers improved these flying machines.

And today we fly any place in the world in less time than it took our great, great grandparents to travel a hundred miles over the

Kansas prairie in their covered wagons.

The town where you live or where you go to school was laid out by pioneer town-builders. How proud they were when the town grew and prospered.

How excited the people in your town were when the railroad arrived.

Yes, every Kansas town is a monument to pioneer town-builders.

There are many, many ways the pioneers prepared the way for you.

The pioneer children in their one-room schools.

The political pioneers who worked hard to secure for Kansas women the right to vote.

The pioneer oilmen who plunged their drills deep into the ground and helped to build a vital Kansas industry.

A Kansas natural gas plant.

In the Garden City cemetery I found a wonderful pioneer story.

"William H. Foster . . . born in England. Came to western Kansas in 1898 and always believed in its future."

Here is the story of a pioneer—one who prepared the way for all of us.

Chapter Twenty-Five: Tomorrow's Pioneers

"In every generation there are pioneers. There were the Kansas pioneers who traveled in covered wagons. And today there are Kansas pioneers who are exploring outer space."

"What kind of pioneer do you want to be? What do you want to do to help prepare the way for the next generation of Kansans?"

"You are going to have to use your imagination now, for you are going to visit a Kansas school of the future. They year is 2025 A.D."

The school building is certainly different from the school buildings of today.

Listen to the teacher talk to the class.

"Today, students, we are going to talk about some

pioneers of the past—the people in our families who lived back in the 1980's and 1990's. Do any of you have some stories about your family pioneers you want to share with us?"

Hands fly up all over the room. The teacher calls on a young lady.

"My grandfather designed an energy efficient house that was needed at that time when there was an energy shortage."

"My dad says that his father invented the solar adapter energizer which was the first step toward developing the solar equipment we have to heat and cool our school and homes today."

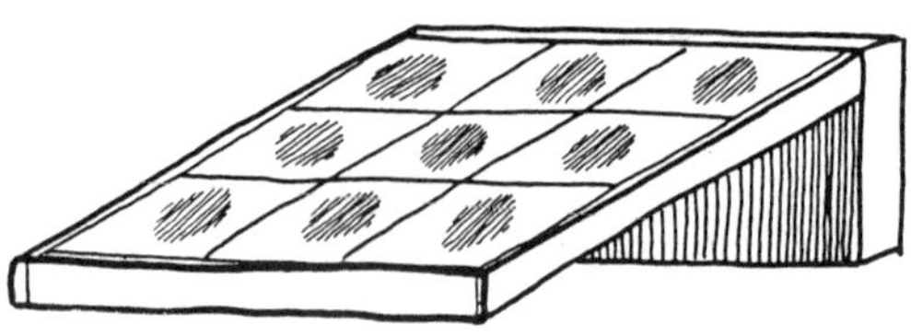

"Speaking of machines—do you know what my Aunt Janet told me? She said that when she went to school they didn't have computer terminals at their desks. Can you imagine anything so dumb?"

All the children laugh at how simply the pioneers lived . . . back in the 1980's.

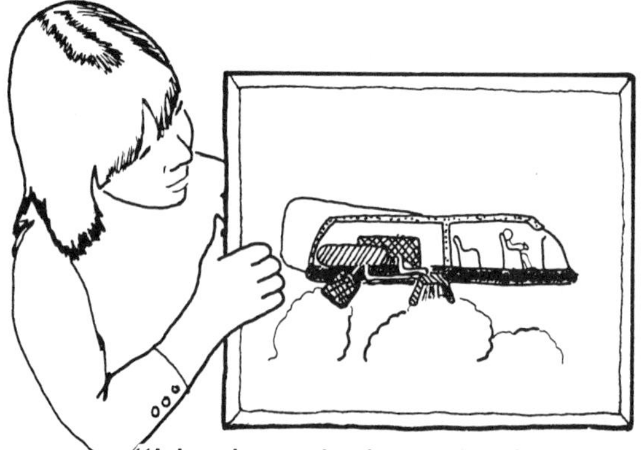

"I had a relative who invented the rocket transporter. It was a simple machine—not at all like our transporters today."

"Somewhere in my family, back at this time, I had an uncle who was a farmer. He invented the earth synthesizer—you know, those remote-controlled machines that plow, plant and fertilize a field in one operation?"

"I'm really proud of one of my ancestors. She discovered cures for many of the diseases which afflicted people back in those days. You and I don't even hear of those diseases today."

"Do you know who these students are talking about?"

"Yes, they are talking about you! Those are your children sitting in the classroom, and they are talking about their family pioneers."

"Take some time to think about your future. You will discover that there are many ways you can become a pioneer."

A Heritage Check List

Make sure you do these things:

✔ 1. Visit the local historical society and find out about where you live.

✔ 2. Find all the historical markers that are near you and discover the stories they have to tell.

✔ 3. Discover the story of all the people who live in your community—the pioneers who have come from many lands.

✔ 4. Listen to the adults whose names are in your People Bank.

HERITAGE SPECIAL HERITAGE SPECIAL HERITAGE SPECIAL HERITAGE SPECIAL

You will discover that your lives today are very different from the ways your parents and grandparents lived.

Do you realize that your children and grandchildren will want to know how you lived . . . back in the "good old days"?

What will you save for your children and grandchildren?

"Let me tell you about OPERATION ATTIC."

Many years ago houses had places called attics. (Perhaps your house still has one.) An attic was a room under the roof where trunks and boxes of old things were stored.

The attic was a wonderful place for children to play. As they searched through the boxes and trunks, they found things that had belonged to their parents and their grandparents.

The "pieces of history" stored away in the attic helped children discover their heritage.

Do you know what? You need to have your very own attic. Why? Because twenty-five years from now your children will be asking you questions:

"Dad, what were you doing when you were my age?"

"Mom, what was school like back then?"

"What did you and your friends do for fun?"

"What did our town look like in those days?"

"How did you farm back then?"

Yes, your children will have many, many questions. And it is important for you to have answers for their questions.

So, why don't you do this.

Take a large envelope. On the outside of the envelope write these words:

TO MY CHILDREN. TO BE OPENED IN THE YEAR _________. You can fill in the blank space with the year you select.

Now you must decide what things you want to save for your children. Can't you just see their faces when they open this envelope and see the things you have saved for them?

For sure you will want to save pictures of you and your friends. Your children will enjoy seeing those photos—and photos of your home and your school, too.

I know one thing that would be exciting for your children: if they could hear your voice.

Look back in Chapter Five. Find the list of questions you asked your parents. Turn on your tape recorder and now **you** answer those very same questions. I know your children will enjoy hearing you talk about yourself.

If you are too shy to use the tape recorder, write the answers to the questions on a piece of paper. Your children will enjoy reading your answers.

The photographs, tape cassettes and written stories your children find in their attics will help them understand that they are a part of history.

And what fun they will have learning about your life back in "the good, old days."

I want to thank you for reading my book. And I want to wish you all the best of luck, as you follow the pioneer trails of Kansas.

Your friend

Robert Manley

Dr. Robert Manley

"Best of luck to all you future Kansas pioneers!"

Photo Credits

All pictures are from the collections of the Kansas State Historical Society except as follows:

Nebraska State Historical Society

58
61
62 Upper
62 upper
66 upper left
66 lower right
79
128 lower
164 lower right
173
175 left
206 upper right

St. Louis Missouri Public Library

Page No. 77

Dickinson County Historical Society - Abilene

Page No. 126 upper right
130 upper left
130 upper right
134 upper
137 lower left
137 lower right
164 upper left
184 lower right
195 left
207 lower right

Meade County Historical Society - Meade

Page No. 129 lower right
131 upper right
147 lower
148 upper right

Hodgeman County Historical Society - Jetmore

Page No. 130 lower right
145 upper left

Kiowa County Historical Society - Greensburg

Page No. 138 upper left

Republic County Historical Society - Belleville

Page No. 147 upper
207 upper left
207 upper right
208 upper left

Kansas City Museum - Kansas City, Missouri

Page No. 207 middle left